COOL TOBACCO, SWEET COCA

COOL TOBACCO, SWEET COCA

Teachings of an Indian Sage from the Colombian Amazon

A bilingual edition of
Jírue Dɨona, Rɨérue Jɨibina

Narrated in the Uitoto language by
Hipólito Candre "Kɨneraɨ"

Translated from the Uitoto, and with a commentary by
Juan Alvaro Echeverri

THEMIS BOOKS

This edition first published
in 1996 by Themis Books, an imprint of
Green Books, Foxhole, Dartington,
Totnes, Devon TQ9 6EB
in association with the COAMA Programme, Colombia
and The Gaia Foundation, London

Distributed in the USA & Canada by Council Oak Books, Tulsa, Oklahoma

Originally published as *Tabaco frío, coca dulce*
© 1993 by Hipólito Candre and Juan Alvaro Echeverri
(National Award on Indian Oral Literature, Colcultura, Colombia)

English text revised by Jimmy Weiskopf
Line drawings by Andrés Platarrueda
Photographs, unless otherwise indicated, by Olga L. Montenegro

Printed by The Cromwell Press, Broughton Gifford, Wiltshire

The paper used in this book is made from wood from managed plantations,
where replanting exceeds the trees harvested. These are in North America, coastal
areas of Brazil (eucalyptus plantations, harvested every seven years), Portugal and
Spain. The paper is acid-free and elemental chlorine-free.

A catalogue record for this book is available from the British Library

ISBN 0 9527302 1 9

Cover photograph: Hipólito Candre "Kɨnerai"

CONTENTS

5

To
kue mirɨgo Fareka Buinaiño
Olga Lucía Montenegro

INTRODUCTION

These texts are the result of a collaboration between an anthropologist and a biologist who have worked in indigenous territories in the Colombian Amazon and an indigenous elder who is seeking to foster the welfare and growth of his children and family.[1] This alliance was interwoven like a basket in which we now deposit the fruits of this search in the form of texts which were first tape-recorded and then transcribed into written words.

This basket (the written word) is not part of the indigenous world to which Kɨneraɨ, the author of these texts, belongs. This basket is something new, it is like the iron axes which the ancestors of these races obtained from white traders. Those axes, says Kɨneraɨ, were "hot." The elders of that time assembled and examined an axe to determine whether it did the job or not. They saw that it was useful but also that it was dangerous if it was not handled properly. For this reason they used the same Word for it which is used in these texts: the Word of cool tobacco, the Word of sweet coca. Books and writing are like the white man's axe; they are strong, like the axe, but they are also hot. That is why the Word with which this basket is filled is a cool and sweet Word, a Word to care for life. You will not find here stories about cosmogonies or legends of spirits or heroes. Here you will find the Word of life, the seeds of work, the tasks of the mother and the father, the care of children. This is the Word with which Kɨneraɨ fills the basket, thinking of his children, thinking of those who are growing. From this basket we are removing these texts so that they can be known both by white men and the native races. For this reason we publish it in its original indigenous language, Uitoto,[2] and in an English translation.

Who is Kɨneraɨ?

Kɨneraɨ is the name, in Uitoto language, of Hipólito Candre. Through his paternal lineage he is of the Okaina race, but both his mother and the two wives he has had are speakers of Uitoto, and he has lived most of his life among that ethnic group. That is why, although an Okaina, he speaks the Uitoto language, mainly the dialect of the Igarapaná river, which is known as the *mɨnɨka* dialect.

The name Kɨneraɨ means "dry miriti palm." This is the name of an elder; it signifies that the miriti palm which has dried out—so that only the trunk remains—is where the parrot nests and lays a single egg. For this reason although it seems that the palm has died it can still produce new life. This name belongs to the clan of the father of Kɨneraɨ: the *Kɨnere* or Miriti Palm Grove clan of the Okaina people. Due to the fact that his grandparents lived together with the members of the Tiger *(Jiko)* clan, Kinerai calls the clan of his family by its complete name, which is *Jikofo Kinéreni,* "the tiger of the miriti palm grove."

Miriti palm *(Mauritia flexuosa).* Photo by Marta L. Torres

Kinerai was born near Tarapacá, on the Putumayo river, on the Colombo-Brazilian frontier, a few years before the border conflict between Colombia and Peru of 1932-1933. His birth in such a far-off land was part of the great indigenous exodus which resulted from the violence and forced migrations promoted by the rubber companies at the beginning of this century, especially by the notorious Casa Arana. After the conflict between Colombia and Peru, the Igaraparaná river, the traditional homeland of the Uitoto and Okaina groups, was deserted. The establishment of a Capuchin mission in La Chorrera, in the mid-Igaraparaná, stimulated the re-population of the river. In the 1940s, Kinerai's father also decided to return, with his family, to his native land. They first lived in La Chorrera, where Kɨneraɨ received a basic education and got married towards the end of the 1940s. It was then that he began to *mambe* coca.[3] In his own words (the fragments which follow were tape-recorded in Spanish):

> It was then that my father said, you are already married, now you have to *mambe,* you are now going to begin your work; and now, well, [because] you know, for this reason you now have a wife, now you must *mambe.* Well then, he was already *mambeing,* so he now got some coca toasted and got some vegetable salt.[4]
> Then in that *uiyobe* [heliconia] leaf—he brought a fresh leaf from the forest—there he put about two spoonfuls [of coca powder], and in another leaf he put tobacco paste, like this, well prepared, well mixed with vegetable salt from that *jarina* [a palm species] and he conjured a tobacco leaf. Afterwards he was conjuring the coca with tobacco paste. Then he said to me, now it's ready, *mambe!* So that was the first time, then, that I began to *mambe.*
> He had already begun to talk to me, since I already had a wife, to take care of her by myself: here you have to work; when a man marries he has to have a food-plot, he has to have everything and know how to weave a basket, a sieve; you already know this, I can't be telling you what to do; good, now prepare coca on your own, pound it, sieve it; when there isn't any then you have to bring it from the food-plot—he would say. Good, I would say. And so on and so forth. You mustn't sleep, he would say, one sleeps and gets up and licks tobacco and *mambes* a bit [of coca powder] and then you lie down so that you get used to all this, because later on you're going to have a child. Only he didn't say all this at once, but he was always seated there in the *mambeing* place, talking, and I was beside him. That is how we lived and then the first child, my eldest son, was born. Now's the time, he told me, now you have to look after things, now you're going to learn a lot of things; before, when you were on your own, you only ate and slept, but now you're no longer going to sleep like that, I am only going to watch you. So I now only thought about all this that I am telling you. I no longer thought about anything else, I was now really worried about all this. So then, I continued and never stopped *mambeing* to this very day.

Kɨneraɨ had four children by his first marriage, three of whom are still alive. His wife died accidentally towards the end of the 1950s and Kɨneraɨ stayed a widower for ten years, during which he looked after his family on his own. During this period he was working for the missionaries in La Chorrera. He also travelled during that time. He visited other indigenous groups and learned many things—

about healing and about black magic.

Then, towards the end of the 1960s, he got married for the second time, to a niece of his first wife. Kinerai relates:

> Yes, after that, well, I was already living here, so, I no longer left this place to travel far away, but once more the only thing I thought about now was how to sustain my children, how to look after them, so that I would be able to know about the things our grandfather taught us. Whether it was true or false, I would say to myself. So I got down to work and sowed my coca and tobacco, and now that was for looking, for searching well. Because one cannot know just like that, but one must work in order to see, one must prepare tobacco and coca. Because they used to say that this is how one learns, this is how one searches.
>
> But I was no longer with my father; first I lived with my father and later, when I came to live here, I was already on my own. Good, my father would say, he who knows how to work well and prepare [tobacco and coca] well can learn this. So I fulfilled all that. So now I sat down with that tobacco and coca. I no longer thought about anything else, only about what that Word was like, the Word of coca and of tobacco and of sweet manioc and of peanut and of edible manioc and of bitter manioc—all of them. So, from then on, I began to see things really well, I now had to get drunk with that [tobacco and coca] in order to look: is it possible or not? Because they say that there, in tobacco, is the spirit, and that spirit is in coca. So when one looks by himself, then one can say that it *is* there. But what another relates one believes, but you almost cannot believe it. In all this I, well, I had to find out for myself. I was already making vegetable salt, everything, all well prepared. I would get drunk and I would only see, so to speak, the Word of coca, of tobacco. Everything was there, that is, all about peanut, about edible manioc, everything. I only heard the Word, but I wanted to see the spirit of tobacco, of coca. I worried a lot about this. And he [the spirit] would say that I still wasn't ready. So once again I had to get drunk, get drunk by means of the drunkenness of tobacco, so that I could be shown a thing like that, like that. Then, as I already had everything ready in myself, then I would be able to see a thing like that—it looked blue—but then it would get lost again. So I thought, is it that I can't see it like that, or it's not possible? Then, since it is the pure spirit of tobacco, now finally, the tobacco [spirit]—since as they say, you cannot get hold of it that easily

Kɨneraɨ's house

and in all this I took a long time—then the spirit still told me that, the Word of tobacco has not formed in your heart, recite these invocations. But I still hadn't recited this invocation of the spirit of tobacco, then I had to conjure it in tobacco paste and in a leaf of tobacco. Then I thought that it took no more than that to see with this, that I could say that yes, I do have the spirit of tobacco—but it wasn't so. Then I had to conjure the tobacco paste. I now licked it and smoked it, so that it now left my heart, it came out of me like that, it came out sort of green, so that now it was ready, I now do have it. Then the spirit said, well you can now heal your baby, your wife, your children, that invocation is only to care for one's home; now you *can* recite invocations, he told me. And from there on I recited invocations.

Kɨneraɨ settled down in the place where he lives to this day, at the foot of a rocky outcrop near the Igaraparaná river. He continued studying the spirit of tobacco until the second son of his first marriage died in an accident, a young man in his twenties who was his right arm and companion. In that trance the spirit of tobacco showed him an important vision:

After that I was sad once again. So I felt this sadness, this pain, right here. And as they say, well, I was crying, and, well then, thinking. And from thinking so much, in this state the very same

13

spirit that I had then told me [in the drunkenness of tobacco]: why are you crying? He didn't die and you are going to go beyond all that, you must have five sons, he told me—just like that, as though he were a person. Look, he said, you already see tobacco plants here. But, how big those plants were! With a lot of seeds. And in their midst, there was a plant of sweet manioc, only one. There it is, he said, but you aren't going to see it just yet, this takes time. So I thought, when am I going to see it? After that I heard another word saying: you have to look after this now, because you were sort of praying and loved your son a lot and want to have more sons, so you have to look after it; you shouldn't think about problems or be envious; you have to be disciplined about this, there I will see whether you obeyed my word; if you take up the word of anger, of fighting, again, or do anything other than my command, then you're no longer going to live in this world—the spirit told me.

From his second marriage five sons and a daughter were actually born. The tobacco plants that he saw in that vision signified the sons and the plant of sweet manioc—only one—signified his daughter. The tobacco plants he saw were big and full of seeds, which meant that these children would produce many descendants. These children and descendants are what the spirit ordered him to look after.

The work of tape-recording and transcription which we carried out with Kinerai in 1992 originates from that same vision. That same Word for looking after his children is the Word Kinerai is speaking of in these texts. These new children have already grown up and are already producing those new descendants. The first grandson from his second marriage was born in 1992 and the children of his first marriage have already produced six grandchildren. Since those children are already learning the white people's ways, go to school and learn to read, Kinerai sought, with our help, to place that same Word in a book so that it can be passed on to his descendants. The eldest son of his second marriage is training to be a school teacher and has already begun to use the Uitoto transcriptions of these tape-recordings. In his community a bilingual school began to operate in 1993 and that son is its first teacher.

Of the voluminous collection of tape-recordings that we made I have chosen a small selection so that other races and other cultures can know the teachings of Kinerai—the Word of tobacco and coca which Kinerai has achieved through study, endeavor and suffering.

Kinerai further relates:

So it has been from that time to the present day. And I continue studying how to heal the sicknesses that happen. Ah! but not just

14

Kɨneraɨ's wife, Beni, in her kitchen

like that, but with tobacco and coca and the leaf of tobacco. If I had left it like that, without study, I wouldn't have known anything. Like that I went on getting drunk and went as far as I could, because one can't say that I arrived where no one can go, I don't say that, no. I keep up with it and although I'm old, I continue. That is how I learned to do my first healing with tobacco and after that the tobacco cure for hemorrhages, for madness, for tumors, for a person who is skinny or for a woman who has not been able to have a child; all that I learned as well. And to fortify a woman who has always had small babies, and another invocation, and another. So I learned that as well, the invocation for coughing, for fever, all that I have. And to find out what's happening to a child or relation who lives far away, to see into that. And I conjured my eyes [with magic powers]. All that, then, I learned, yes. And since then, up to today, in this I live, thinking about how you can learn another invocation. It may be that there is or isn't one, but it always takes time to know about another invocation. And I do this in the midst of many envies, many problems, but I don't let them affect me. Such is my life.

The Poetic Form of Indigenous Oral Performance

"By translation with a poetic criterion I do not mean
one that is freer or more distant
from the original, but one that is more faithful
to the poetry of the original."
Ernesto Cardenal
Anthology of Primitive Poetry[5]

Indigenous narratives are usually translated in the form of prose. Much of the expressive force of the oral art of Kɨnerai—which derives its strength from the oral art of the culture he belongs to and transmits—is weakened in a prose translation. Such a form of translation obliges one to eliminate or tone down precisely that which is most expressive and notable in his oral art: pauses, interchanges with his conversation partner, reiterations, recurring expressions, the extended listing of things.

To transmit this expressive force I have decided to present these Uitoto texts, as well as their translations, in a poetic form. The quotation from Cardenal expresses what I have tried to achieve, that is, not adapt the translation to a predetermined model of "poetry" in the European or Western sense of the word but rather, to work towards a discovery of the forms of expression inherent in the original texts. This requires the reader to stretch himself or herself, but it offers as a reward the opportunity to get close to the spirit and power of the original. The translation which is given here is an attempt to transmit the form, content and meaning of the texts in the most exact way.

What I call the poetic presentation of the texts is based on three formal elements: lines, verses and stanzas.[6]

Lines

The lines of the text are largely defined by the pauses in the flow of conversation. These pauses are taken advantage of by the conversation partner, who expresses his agreement by saying *jm* or *jɨɨ,* which means "yes." The lines are also marked, in some cases, by parallelism—that is to say, sequences of lines with a similar structure in which one element changes (see the example given below). Each line of the text is printed separately; when a line occupies more than one line it continues, right-justified, on the line below. Each line is given a number which is printed on the right-hand margin of the page at intervals of five lines. These numbers allow the reader to compare the Uitoto text with the translation and refer to the texts cited in the commentary.

An example of parallelism, which also serves to illustrate what a typical line is made up of, can be found in text 2 (lines 8-26). I reproduce, here, the Uitoto text

16

followed by its English translation. In the translation the replies of the conversation partner are omitted:

Fia ua jagɨ́yɨna ite,   *jm* jɨ́
  farékatofe jagɨyɨ,   *jm*
  juzítofe jagɨyɨ,   *jm*   10
  rozídoro jagɨyɨ,   *jm*
  mazákarɨ jagɨyɨ,   *jm*
  jífikue jagɨyɨ,   *jm*
  jɨrɨ́kue jagɨyɨ,   *jm*
  jizaiño jagɨyɨ,   *jm*   15
  mɨzena jagɨyɨ,   *jm*
  jimedo jagɨyɨ,   *jm*
  tuburɨ jagɨyɨ,   *jm*
  jakaijɨ jagɨyɨ,   *jm*
  dunajɨ jagɨyɨ,   *jm*   20
  mɨzena jagɨyɨ,   *jm* jm
  jifirai jagɨyɨ,   *jm* jm
  nekana jagɨyɨ,   *jm*
  goido jagɨyɨ,   *jm*
  nemona jagɨyɨ,   *jm* jm *jm* jm *jm* jm   25
  nana fia jagɨ́yɨna ite.   *jm* jm

The translation is as follows. Kɨnerai is speaking about the breath which is to be found in the womb of the Working Mother:

There is only breath,
  breath of sweet manioc,
  breath of bitter manioc,   10
  breath of pineapple,
  breath of peanut,
  breath of sapote,
  breath of forest grape,
  breath of inga,   15
  breath of cacao,
  breath of peach palm,
  breath of *daledale,*
  breath of yam,
  breath of cocoyam,   20
  breath of cacao,
  breath of chili,
  breath of green *umari,*
  breath of black *umari,*

17

breath of yellow *umari*   25
—everything is only breath.

When reading the translation one should allow for a pause after each line. In the Uitoto version, the *jm*'s of the conversation partner appear in italics while those of Kɨneraɨ are shown in Roman type. In most cases, the conversation partner—an essential ingredient of indigenous oral art—was his son Blas.[7]

The length of the lines gives an indication of the tempo—that is, the rhythm and speed of the conversation. A succession of short lines, as in the excerpt given above, indicates a slow tempo—there are many pauses and replies from the conversation partner. Long lines indicate a more accelerated rhythm—there are fewer pauses. This is an exact rendering of the Uitoto version, but this is not so in the translation, since it is very difficult to adjust the length of the translated lines to their Uitoto originals.

Verses

A verse is made up of one or more lines. A line of text seldom corresponds to a complete sentence, but all of the verses are sentences. The verses are characterized by the way they are intoned, usually with a falling pitch at the end. The first line of a verse begins at the left-hand margin; the following line or lines are indented one pica. The excerpt given above, for example, is a verse. It is a particularly long one. Nevertheless, the way of intoning this verse of 23 lines is similar to that of a verse of 2 lines—Kɨneraɨ maintains the same tone of voice in the 21 lines that list the breath of the different plants and only descends in the last one.

The different ways of indenting the lines in the verses reflect peculiarities of his intonation. The most common form of verse is that which shows the first line on the left-hand margin, followed by one or more similarly indented lines; such is the case of the example cited above. But there are other verse forms, for example, that found in text 4 (lines 53-57):

Ja
  eirɨgo
    ie jito   55
      jɨibie béeɨyena nogo
        nite.   *jm* jɨɨ

Now
  the old woman
    makes a pot   55
      to toast the leaves of coca
        for her son.

This "ladder"-type presentation tries to reproduce what might be a single line

Kɨnerai and his son Blas

of text were it not for the fact that it is broken up by short pauses. It is worth noting that the conversation partner only replies after the last line.

The same example serves to illustrate a minor problem which derives from this form of presentation. In many cases the translation requires the original order of the words to be altered, given that English syntax is different from that of Uitoto. Since a sentence may extend over several lines, you then encounter a situation where the translation does not always correspond line by line to the Uitoto text. In the above example the last line, "for her son," is not the translation of "nite"—if we attempt to make the two versions literally coincide, we would have to translate the three last lines as follows: "for her son / a pot for toasting coca / she makes."

Punctuation in Uitoto is also different from punctuation in English. As a general rule, I omit the use of quotation marks and question and exclamation marks in the Uitoto version, but they do appear in the translation. One orthographic sign which I have widely used in the translation are dashes (—); these are used within a verse to indicate breaks in the syntax but only when the intonation does not indicate a change of verses. These dashes are not used in the Uitoto version.

Stanzas

The stanzas are made up of a limited number of verses, usually not more than
five. The stanzas group together verses which are similar for formal reasons or
because of their content. At times the beginning of a stanza is marked by certain
recurring expressions, such as: *Ie jira mei,* "Well then"; *Meita,* "And thus";
amongst many others. It is also common to find that, in the division of stanzas,
the pauses are longer or there is a greater exchange of *jm*'s with the conversation
partner. In several texts the stanzas tend to group together a similar number of
verses: four or five of them, usually interwoven with stanzas of two or three
verses. Some stanzas are long, for example the stanza which runs from line 115
to 137 in text 3, which contains ten verses. The division between stanzas is
shown, on the page, by a blank line.

Sections and Parts

In addition to the three elements—lines, verses and stanzas—which represent
formal characteristics inherent in the texts, I have, in some cases, marked out
bigger units of division, which I call sections and parts. A section of a text is made
up of a number of stanzas which deal with a particular theme; and the parts group
together sections or divide the body of the text in terms of contents, intention or
style. The reasons for such divisions can be found in the commentaries on the
respective texts. The identification of these sections and parts is a tool which I
use to help the reader to understand the overall organization of the material, but
other divisions—or none at all—might be equally valid. For this reason I have
chosen a discreet way of indicating them, on the right-hand margin of the page:
the sections with lower-case Roman numerals and the parts with upper-case
Roman numerals.

The Texts and Their Translation

A total of 16 texts are presented. Nine of the texts, which are numbered
continuously with Arabic numerals, make up the major body of the work. Except
for the first and the last, this body of material was tape-recorded with Kinerai
during a one-week period and in the order in which it is presented.[8] These texts
constitute his explanations of the fundamental principles of the Word of tobacco
and coca: the work of the food-plot (text 2), the education of the young men (text
3), the Word of tobacco to conjure the heart of the people (text 4), the Word of
strength (text 5), the Word for cooling down (text 6), the work of the mother (text
7), and the work of the father (text 8).

Text 1, which was recorded several months after the ones I have just
mentioned, contains a tight synthesis of the major points which the other major

texts develop; and text 9, which ends the collection, was recorded at the end of the work and offers some reflections on Kɨneraɨ's own life which serve to recapitulate all that has gone before.

Interwoven between this series of major texts I have included a series of complementary texts which amplify, explain and illustrate certain points which are treated in a brief or metaphorical way in the major texts. These texts are marked by the number of the major text which they complement, followed by a letter.

The major series of texts illustrates what Kɨneraɨ calls "the conversation of tobacco." This conversation does not deal with myths or history; it is the Word with which Kɨneraɨ searches for knowledge and ensures that his work is complete: the work of the food-plot and looking after the welfare of his family. The complementary texts, on the other hand, show other styles of conversation. Two of them are traditional narratives: the dreams of abundance (text 2B)— which, according to Kɨneraɨ, is a continuation of the Uitoto myth "The tree of abundance"—and the story of the giant armadillo (text 3A). Three of the complementary texts are explanations of the invocations of tobacco: the invocation for the pregnant mother (text 2A), the invocation for cooling down tobacco (text 6A), and the invocation for the child who sleeps restlessly (text 6B); the last one also contains the text of this same invocation along with a musical transcription of the chant. Finally, another two complementary texts contain more personal stories which are drawn from Kɨneraɨ's life and which he uses to illustrate certain points: the way in which he "cleaned" the place where he settled down (text 3B) and a story which has to do with the conjuring of his eyes with magical powers (text 8A).

All of the transcriptions are presented whole, without eliminating a single word.[9] All of the texts are, as well, complete narratives which have a beginning and an end; they are not fragments of longer narrations or conversations. The transcription is phonemic—that is, it represents phonemes, not sounds—and it uses the Uitoto spelling that was adopted in the indigenous teacher-training courses in La Chorrera (Amazonas, Colombia), which is explained in a note which follows this introduction.

The translation has the same number of lines as the original and reproduces the form of the verses and stanzas of the original. The translation is a free one but closely follows the Uitoto original. The words which I have added to give more coherence to the translation have been placed between square brackets.

For the translation of texts 3A, 4 and 9 I have relied on preliminary translations into Spanish prepared with the help of one of Kɨneraɨ's sons, and for texts 2B and 3B I have relied on translations done by Olga Lucía Montenegro, who shared this work with me; the other texts were translated by me. The Spanish translation of texts 1, 2, 2A, 2B, 3, 3A and 3B was revised by Argemiro Candre, a son of

Kɨneraɨ, after the publication of the Uitoto-Spanish version of this book. The English version of these texts, as presented here, is *not* the translation of the Spanish version. The texts were completely translated from the Uitoto original, maintaining the Spanish version as a reference.

As well as our field notes, I made use of the Uitoto teaching grammar and the Uitoto-Spanish dictionary published by Eugene and Dorothy Minor (1982, 1987) of the Summer Institute of Linguistics, and of the Uitoto-German dictionary prepared by Konrad T. Preuss (1921-1923) in his outstanding work on Uitoto religion and mythology.[10]

The commentaries on the translation are extensive notes which serve to guide the reading of the texts. They include commentaries by Kɨneraɨ which help to clear up difficult points, establish relationships between various texts, place certain information within its proper context, discuss formal questions having to do with verse forms and the way the texts are presented, and insofar as it is relevant, discuss linguistic and anthropological questions without using a technical or specialized language.

The appendices show the biological names for all of the animals and plants mentioned in the texts and commentaries. Appendix 1 deals with cultivated plants, appendix 2 with other plant species, and appendix 3 with animal species. The biological classification of these species is the result of the detailed and expert labor by the biologist Olga Lucía Montenegro. The botanist Liliana Rosero kindly helped to classify several of the plant species.

The task of translation

Uitoto Spelling

Vowels (6):

i $ɨ$ u

e o

a

Consonants (18):

p b t d ch y k g h

f v z j

m n $ñ$ $ǥ$

r

Long vowels are represented by a duplication of the symbol.

Most common diphthongs and triphthongs:

ai ei oi ue ui uai uei
aɨ eɨ oɨ ua ɨi uaɨ ueɨ

All of the syllables are open. The accent is indicated by placing the accent mark (´) over the vowel of the syllable that carries the accent. The accent is not placed on grave words except to break up a diphthong, for example: *ñúe, úai.*

Guide to Pronunciation

The vowels are pronounced approximately as they are in Spanish or Italian and the consonants have their standard values, with the following exceptions and additions:

$ɨ$ is a high central vowel; it is pronounced by placing the tongue in the position of *u* and the lips in the position of *i;*

p, t, k must be pronounced without aspiration;

ch sounds like in English "church";

y sounds like in English "judge";

h indicates a glottal pause;

f sounds like a *p* pronounced without completely closing the lips;

v sounds like a *b* pronounced without completely closing the lips;

z sounds like *th* in "thin";

j sounds like in Spanish "juez" (stronger than *h* in "hat");

ñ sounds like *ñ* in Spanish, or like *gn* in French;

ǥ is a nasal velar consonant; it sounds like *ng* in "long";

r sounds like in Spanish "arena," not like in English "rare."

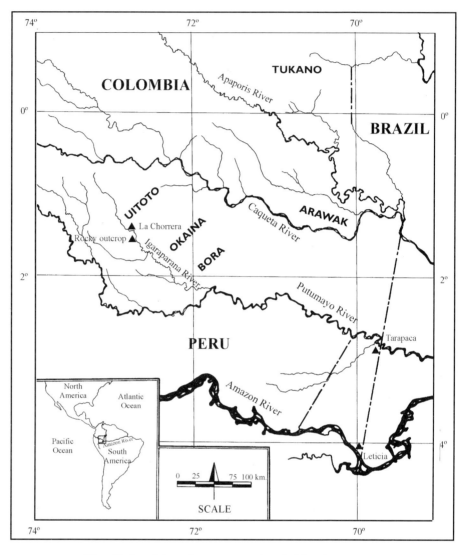

The Colombian Amazon and neighboring areas

THE TRUE SEED

Bibe 1
Ua ijɨ ritɨmɨe

Ero káɨmakɨ.
Buu mei úa ñuera rafue arɨ atɨdɨmɨe,
  nɨɨ ráfuena onódɨmɨe,
  nɨɨ rafue ua yoraɨma.
Nɨɨ ráfuena onódɨmɨe,   5
  nɨeze eróikana
  onode.
Nɨeze eróikana ñúe rafue kɨoide
  daɨdɨmɨe.

Ie jira   10
  mei uina kɨódɨmɨe
    mei buu uina kɨoiye,
  nɨɨ jefona kakáidɨmɨe.
Imɨe onoiga,
  ímɨemona bairede.   15
Nɨgafue atɨde,
  nɨgafue yote.
Onóiñegafue atɨde,
  onóiñegafue yote.

Ɨna fui   20
  baɨna onoiye,
    daɨde.
Ɨna fui
  baɨna kakáiye.
Ɨna fui   25
  baɨna kɨóitɨo.
Ɨna fui
  raɨre arɨ rafue biñede,
  raɨre arɨ rafue kɨóiñena.

26

Text 1

The Planter of the True Seed

Look at our people.
Who is the one who brings the good Word,
  the one who understands that Word,
  the one who imparts that Word?
The one who understands that Word,   5
  how did he
  learn?
What is the good Word like?
  And he who carries it through?

Now then,   10
  the one whose eye sees,
  —and whose eye will see?
  the same whose ear listens.
He knows it,
  it shines forth in him.   15
What news does he bring?
  What news does he tell?
He brings things unknown,
  he tells things unknown.

"Later on   20
  it will be known,"
    it says.
"Later on
  it will be heard."
"Later on   25
  you will see it."
"Later on—
  true Things do not appear at once,
  true Things are not seen at once."

Nɨɨa uido kɨóiñena,   30
  fia dofodo kakade,
  fia jefodo kadade (daɨde),
  jagíyɨna kakade.
Nɨɨ rafue jenódɨmɨe,
  nɨɨ rafue jiyakɨ méiñotɨmɨe,   35
  nɨɨ rafue yoye
  daɨdímɨe.
Ie báɨfene
  fui úa rafue mózikaite.
Ie báɨfene   40
  úa ráfuena kɨóitɨo.

Ja ua fuite.
Jae dofodo
  kakade, jefodo.

Ie yezika jae   45
  ua kaɨ naɨ onóiñena yezika onódɨmɨe,
  kaɨ naɨ kɨóñena yezika kɨódɨmɨe.
Fia ie úai,
  fia ie komekɨ.
                                                            [II]
Ie izoi eróikano,   50
  naɨ fia taɨno uaina ite.
Fui, nɨnomo afeno
  baɨ batɨnomo onóitɨo,
  baɨ batɨnomo kɨóitɨo.
Ie jira afénori,   55
  jae moo yɨɨnota
    akɨ daɨi ja mozíñoga
    mei íena kaɨ kɨódɨkaɨ,
  kɨódɨkaɨ íadɨ
    mei naɨ oni kaɨ ua   60
  yɨɨnoñedɨkaɨ.
Yɨɨnotɨmɨemona bairede,
  yɨɨnoñedɨmɨemona bainide.

28

"The eye does not see it,   30
  only the nose feels it,
  only the ear feels it,
  it feels like breath."
Such is the seeker of that Word,
  such is he who looks into the root of that Word,   35
  such is the sayer
  of teachings.
"Further ahead,
  later, it will stand as a true Thing."
"Further ahead   40
  you will see it as a true Thing."

It finished speaking.
The nose already
  felt, so did the ear.

Before,   45
  when we still did not know, he knew,
  when we still did not see, he saw.
Only his word,
  only his heart.

      [II]
In the same way,   50
  these are yet only empty words.
Then, how
  will you learn later on,
  how will you see later on?
Now then, for that reason the children will later say: 55
  "Our father before us received it,
    in this way he made it stand,
    and then we saw it;
  and although we have seen it
    we did not receive it   60
    on our own."
It shines forth in he who received it,
  it does not shine forth in those who did not receive it.

Ie jira, afeno akie izóikano arɨ
   ja mei uáfuena monáidena kaɨ kɨódɨkaɨ.   65
Ie mei jae kɨóñena,
   ite íadɨ.
Ie jira,
   ja ua mei afe uaido yetaka úrue fui komúiadɨ
   aféfuena kɨoite,   70
   aféfuena ja kakaite.
Meita,
   iñede omoɨ dáɨitate,
   ite.

Meita fia ua,   75
   akie izoi mamékɨ-
   -na kakádɨmɨe
   iñede daɨnánona,
   ja ua, faɨnókaiya
   méinomo ja arɨ bite.   80
Daɨnáfuena itɨno.

Commentary on Text 1:

"THE PLANTER OF THE TRUE SEED"

Rafue is the Uitoto term I translate as "Word" in the first stanza.[1] Further below I translate it as "Thing."[2] However, *rafue* refers neither to words nor to things, *rafue* is the activity through which words are turned into things—the movement from the named to the real through time. The two roots that compose the term— *raa*, "a thing," and *ifue*, "something spoken"—synthesize this movement. When the activity of *rafue* just begins, it manifests itself as words—the naming of what is sought; towards the end of the activity, it manifests itself as things—the things that are sought (food, game, offspring).

   When one asks a Uitoto person about the meaning of the term *rafue*, the most frequent answer is "dance ritual." Dance rituals are *rafue* because, during a few weeks, people can witness how what at the beginning was just talk, at the end

Now then, in this way we have seen
  that this has already dawned as a true Thing.   65
And, although it was not seen before
  it does exist.
Now then,
  in truth, if a child is brought up with that word
  the child will see that Word,   70
  the child will listen to that Word.
And so,
  you may say it does not exist,
  but it does exist.

And so,   75
  he who only listens to its name
  saying that there is nothing
  leaves it aside.
  And what is left aside
  later sprouts.   80
This is what there is to tell.

---

is received as food, game, tobacco, coca.[3] *Rafue* is not just the words of the ritual; if those words do not generate things they are just *bakaki,* "stories." The dance rituals instruct people about the creative power of that Word. That is why it is also admissible to translate *rafue* as "teaching."

Kɨneraɨ frequently refers to his speeches as *rafue*. He explains: "This is not the Word of dance rituals, but it is *rafue*; people believe that *rafue* is only dance ritual, but this is because they don't understand." The Word of dance rituals seeks Things, mainly food, to gladden the people, but Kɨneraɨ's Word is *komúiyafue,* that is, "Word of life." This Word seeks people's growth—new offspring, new generations. Such a Word does not "dawn" (manifest itself as Things) quickly, as the Word of dance rituals does.

The Word of life does not deal with cosmogonies, or myths of origin, as the Word of dance rituals does. As what it seeks is people's growth, it begins with the Word of food *(guiyafue)*. Once there is food, then the baskets (people) appear, and they need the Word of healing *(zegórafue)* and the Word of hunting *(jiefue)*. Only then—when there are people, food, and game—can one seek the Word of dance rituals *(rafue)* and the myths *(jaiagai,* "the thread of the ancients").

Because Kɨnerai sees that today's Indians have lost their way, he does not want to talk about dance rituals, he does not want to tell myths. He decides to start by seeking the foundations of the Word of life, *komúiyafue*.

That is why he starts by saying: "Look at our people" and asking about *the one* who can bring and explain the Word of life. He is talking about more than a person here, he is also referring to a spiritual presence. Through rhetorical questions (lines-2-9) he is invoking that spirit, asking it to manifest itself.

Next, in the second stanza, he names this spirit as the one "whose eye sees" and "whose ear listens." This form of calling the spirit is common in Kɨnerai's speech. He names it as the ear and the eye of an alert hunter who is able to search and find. The "game" that is now being sought is the same Word of life. The other verses continue referring to that same spirit; it is the one who is going to bring and tell "things unknown."

In the third stanza that spirit starts to speak (lines-20-29). It makes four statements, all starting with the expression "Later on." *Rafue* requires time to fully manifest itself, that is what the spirit is talking about: "Later on— / true Things do not appear at once, / true things are not seen at once" (lines 27-29). Here I translate *rafue* as Things, that is, the Word that actualizes itself in a tangible form, as food, game, offspring.

This spirit keeps talking in the fourth stanza, but now it refers to the manner in which that Word is received. That Word is subtle, is not visible, "it feels like breath" (line 33). The last two sentences of this stanza allude to the future and promise that this Word will stand and be seen as a "true Thing."

The action of "forming" is expressed by the verb *mózikaide* (line 39) which means "to stop, to hold, to stand." In a larger sense one can interpret it as "to take shape, to form." A living creature exists because it is able to "stop" the flow of the world (food, air) and form it into body, blood, living tissue. The verb *mózikaide* expresses the very activity of *rafue*: the actualization of the spoken into real things—the power by which words stop and stand. In the following texts, it will be clear that the Word of life is "stopped" by means of work and creation, whose paradigms are agricultural work and the formation of a child in the mother's womb. When the Word is stopped it can be witnessed as "a true Thing."

Kɨnerai announces, in the fifth stanza, that the spirit ceased to speak (lines 42-44):

> It finished speaking.
> The nose already
>   felt, so did the ear.

This ends part I in which the tobacco spirit spoke about three things: (1) that the

32

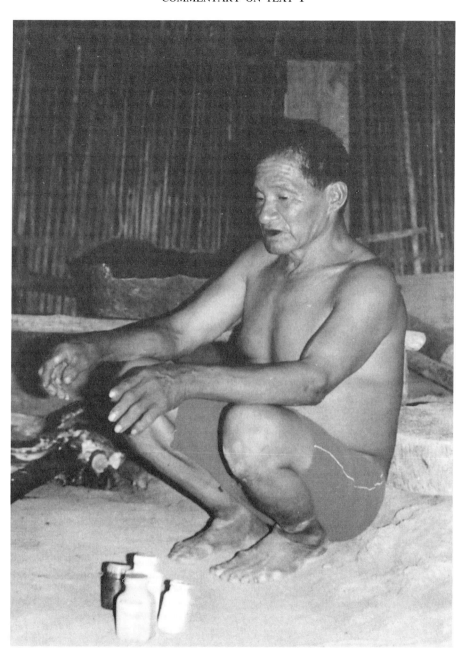

Uttering *rafue*

Things of the Word of life need time to form themselves (lines 20-29), (2) that those Things of life are subtle, like the sensation of breath (lines 30-33), and (3) that when they form they can finally be seen (lines 38-41). The model to understand this process is given in the title of the text, "The Planter of the True Seed." A seed is small and subtle, it is like talk, it is just the promise of something future. It has to be put into the world and needs time to develop. When it finally develops, what it contained first as a promise is then witnessed as a tree and fruits, as something real.

In part II, Kinerai offers a teaching for future generations. It is not the spirit who speaks now but Kinerai himself. He starts by saying: "In the same way / these are yet only empty words" (lines 50-51). When *rafue* starts, there is the danger that the Word be only "empty words" that will not form true Things of life, that will not turn into actualities—"just conversation." The difference between "just conversation" and proper *rafue* is that the one who produces that Word has already demonstrated that he or she is capable of carrying it through. Kinerai then presents himself as one who is able to keep his Word (see lines 62-63). His children and grandchildren will know that that Word is true, because they have seen its works (see lines 55-61).

Kinerai says that although it seems that the Word of life does not exist, he does have the seed and he is planting it again. And if one works with the youngsters that seed will sprout again.

And if we want to believe, as many, that it is lost, we should re-read where he says (lines 72-81):

And so,
   you may say it does not exist,
   but it does exist.
And so,
   he who only listens to its name
   saying that there is nothing,
   leaves it aside.
   And what is left aside
   later sprouts.
This is what there is to tell.

The Mother's Womb

Bibe 2
Tátjɨe jénua úai

[I]

Ie jira mei,
  eiño
  ua jieño.   *jm* jm
Eiño jieño
  eromo ua   5
  ite   *jm*
  jagɨyɨ.   *jm* jm
Fia ua jagɨ́yɨna ite,   *jm* jɨ̈
  farékatofe jagɨyɨ,   *jm*
  juzítofe jagɨyɨ,   *jm*   10
  rozídoro jagɨyɨ,   *jm*
  mazákarɨ jagɨyɨ,   *jm*
  jífikue jagɨyɨ,   *jm*
  jɨrɨ́kue jagɨyɨ,   *jm*
  jizaiño jagɨyɨ,   *jm*   15
  mɨzena jagɨyɨ,   *jm*
  jimedo jagɨyɨ,   *jm*
  tuburɨ jagɨyɨ,   *jm*
  jakaijɨ jagɨyɨ,   *jm*
  dunajɨ jagɨyɨ,   *jm*   20
  mɨzena jagɨyɨ,   *jm* jm
  jifirai jagɨyɨ,   *jm* jm
  nekana jagɨyɨ,   *jm*
  goido jagɨyɨ,   *jm*
  nemona jagɨyɨ,   *jm* jm *jm* jm *jm* jm   25
  nana fia jagɨ́yɨna ite.   *jm* jm

Ie fui baɨ batɨ́nomo   *jm*
  ja ua
  tátjɨena mei
  maménuanona   *jm*   30
  ja ua razíyaɨna ua

Text 2
Seeking out the Garden Work

[I]

Now then,
  the Mother
  is Working Mother.
In the womb
  of the Working Mother   5
  there is
  breath.
There is only breath,
  breath of sweet manioc,
  breath of bitter manioc,   10
  breath of pineapple,
  breath of peanut,
  breath of sapote,
  breath of forest grape,
  breath of inga,   15
  breath of cacao,
  breath of peach palm,
  breath of *daledale,*
  breath of yam,
  breath of cocoyam,   20
  breath of cacao,
  breath of chili,
  breath of green *umari,*
  breath of black *umari,*
  breath of yellow *umari*   25
  —everything is only breath.

Later on, further ahead,
  —truly—
  after having
  resolved to work,   30
  one already has

ja ua ite. *jm*
Dɨnomo fui,
  eiño jieño *jm*
  eromo ite jagɨyɨ ja jino 35
  ja ie oye. *jm*
Dɨnomo ja ua jagɨyɨna jae ite ua, *jm*
  ja jakáizairai jino ie oga, *jm*
  dunajɨ jino ie oga, *jm*
  jifirai jino ie oga, *jm* 40
  mazákarɨ jino ie oga, *jm*
  rozídoro jino ie oga, *jm*
  mɨzedo jino ie oga, *jm*
  jimedo jino ie oga, *jm*
  jɨrɨ́kue jino ie oga, *jm* 45
  jífikue *jm*
    jagɨyɨ *jm*
      jino ie oga. *jm* jm *jm*

Ja ie baɨ batɨ́nomo,
  ja ua 50
  ja mei ua ja ua jakáizairaina ite, *jm*
  tubúrɨna ite, *jm* jɨɨ
  goizédona ite, *jm* jm *jm*
  enokakiyɨna ite, *jm* jm
  bedɨ́gona ite, *jm* jm 55
  chɨkɨpírana ite, *jm* jm
  ja jiménana ite, *jm* jm
  rozídorona ite. *jm* jm
Ja ua, jino *jm*
  oni farékatofena ja ie oga. *jm* jm 60
Ja nana jino ie oga. *jm*

Ie méinori,
  eiño ja jiyode. *jm* jm
Jae baie ua jagɨyɨ eromo ua zegore ite. *jm* jm
Nɨɨ kaɨ komuiya jiyakɨ. *jm* jm 65
Báiena nano urúnaite *jm*

38

a slashed jungle clearing.
There later,
  the breath that was
  in the Working Mother's womb   35
  will be harvested.
Thus, the breath that was—in truth—
  is now harvested as yam,
  is harvested as cocoyam,
  is harvested as chili,   40
  is harvested as peanut,
  is harvested as pineapple,
  is harvested as cacao,
  is harvested as peach palm,
  is harvested as forest grape,   45
  the breath
    of sapote
      is harvested.

Now, further ahead,
  —truly—   50
  now then in truth there is yam,
  there is *daledale,*
  there is yam bean,
  there is taro,
  there is canna lily,   55
  there is arrowroot,
  now there is peach palm,
  there is pineapple.
Now, furthermore
  sweet manioc is harvested,   60
Now, everything is harvested.

Following that,
  the Mother gets well.
That breath she had inside was a flatulence.
That is the very origin of our life.   65
With that, in the beginning, the Mother,

eiño   *jm*
  jieño.   *jm* jm *jm*
Akie izóikana ite.   *jm*

[II]

Afe eróikana ja,   70
  kirigaɨ komuide,   *jm*
  ja kirítikoɨ komuide,   *jm* jm
  ja jebogaɨ komuide,   *jm* jm
Ja ua jíibitikoɨ jíibie oyena,   *jm* jɨɨ
  ja aidóriyagaɨ   *jm* jm   75
  ja komuide.   *jm* jm
Akie izoi   *jm*
  arɨ ja
  ua afe úai bite.   *jm* jm

Mei táɨnomona ua   80
  yónide.   *jm* jm
Afe iya eróikana ja mei
  ja komuide.   *jm*
Ja ua ranita komuide,   *jm*
  yokofe komuide,   *jm* jm   85
  ja jebogaɨ komuide.   *jm* jm
Nɨɨ ñuera úai
  ja ua monaide.   *jm*
Akie izoide.   *jm*

Akɨ dɨnona mei baɨ   90
  fia afe úai
  mei ja baie ua ñuéfuena fakade,   *jm* jm
  fia uaina ja.   *jm*
Akɨ dɨnori arɨ
  ua ja mei monaide,   *jm*   95
  ja kɨona.   *jm* jm

the Working Mother,
   was pregnant.
So it is.

                                                              [II]

With regard to that,   70
   the basket appeared;
   now the little basket appeared,
   now the open-weave basket appeared,
Now the little basket to collect coca leaves,
   now the big basket to harvest manioc tubers   75
   now appeared.
In that manner
   that word
   arose.

But out of nothing   80
   there is nothing to tell.
Considering that there is now [food]
   thus [those things] now appeared.
Now the manioc sieve appeared,
   the manioc strainer appeared,   85
   now the open-weave basket appeared.
That same good word
   now truly dawned.
So it is.

From now on   90
   only this conversation,
   since it was already proved as a good Word
   —only the word.
Up to this point
   it dawned,   95
   now it was seen.

Bibe 2A
Urue komuiya jɨɨra
fia uaina ja

Eiño fueñe jeraimo[1]
  úrue jóobikaiya fakaize   *jm*
  iékoni keiño ɨrábide.   *jm*
Keiño nobɨde,   *jm*
  dɨona jáfaikɨri   *jm*   5
  jɨfaide.   *jm*
Ie fakaize moo buinaima   *jm*
  naino jenode,   *jm*
  jɨbúidemo
  naie jɨɨramo érokaide.   *jm*   10

Naie jɨɨrado
  farékai imugu
  naie jɨɨrado fakade.   *jm*
Ja náiedo eiño jirótate.   *jm*
Iékoni keiño komékɨmo ite   15
  reɨkɨ jafáikɨri
  keiño duere zefuide.   *jm*
Uébikaide   *jm*
  reɨkɨ jáfaikɨri ja.
Dane keiño farékaiño   20
  komekɨ arɨ zúuide.   *jm*

Dɨnori keiño mamekɨ   *jm*
  zúuiya buinaiño.   *jm*
Dɨnori oni
  keiño mamekɨ naɨmekɨ buinaiño.   *jm*   25
Arɨ keiño ja ráɨnadate.   *jm*
Nɨɨ keiño jɨɨra,   *jm*
  moo buinaima fakaka jɨɨra.   *jm* jm
Akɨ náinomona arɨ
  keiño ja arɨ mózikaide.   *jm*   30

Invocation for the Pregnant Mother
—only the word—

When in the mother's womb
  a child first starts to form,
  the mother begins to feel ill.
The mother gets breathless,
  she gets drunk   5
  with the breath of tobacco.
In that moment the Father Buinaima
  begins to inquire,
  and upon examining
  he turns to this spell.   10

With that spell
  he conjures a little juice of sweet manioc—
  with that spell he conjures it.
Now, with that, he makes the mother drink.
Right there the mother was tormented   15
  with the breath of fire
  that was in her heart.
She was burning herself
  with the breath of fire.
Again, the heart of the Mother   20
  of Sweet Manioc is relieved.

After that, the mother's name
  is Mother of Relief.
After that, furthermore,
  the mother's name is Mother of Sweetness.   25
The mother now settles down.
This is the healing spell for the mother,
  the spell that Father Buinaima employed.
From then on
  the mother stands up well.   30

Mózikaiyanona
  arɨ moo buinaima   *jm*
  manaɨde jáfaikɨdo   *jm*
  keiño fúunote.   *jm*
Iékoni   35
  keiño komekɨ
  zuitade jafaikɨ,   *jm*
  dɨno arɨ
  jae farékatofena mózikaide.   *jm*
Keiño joreño   *jm*   40
  oni mazákarɨna mózikaide.   *jm*
Keiño zúuiya buinaiño   *jm*
  akɨ dɨnomo ja
  jae mózikaide.   *jm*
Akie izoide.   *jm*   45

Akɨ dɨnómona
  nane abɨdo
  keiño moo buinaima   *jm*
  komékɨmo reɨkɨ jafaikɨ.   *jm*
Iékoni   50
  moo buinaima
  dɨona jíibina jagɨyɨ,
  keiño dɨnena
  naie jɨɨrado   *jm*
  moo buinaima firáiñote.   *jm*   55
Iékoni
  naie jafáikɨdo firáiñoga   *jm*
  moo komekɨ   *jm*
  naɨménaite,   *jm*
  manánaite.   *jm*   60
Dɨnómona
  moo mamekɨ   *jm*
  jírue dɨona,   *jm*
  rɨérue jíibina.   *jm*
Akie izóikana arɨ fuite.   *jm*   65

When she already stands up well
  the Father Buinaima
  blows over the mother
  with a cool breath.
At once,   35
  the breath released
  by the mother's heart,
  there
  took the form of the plant of sweet manioc.
The mother's spirit,   40
  furthermore, took the form of the plant of peanut.
The Mother of Relief
  in this way
  took form.
So it is.   45

From then on
  once again
  in Father Buinaima's heart
  there is breath of fire.
At once,   50
  the mother herself
  cures Father Buinaima
  with this spell,
  she cures the breath of tobacco and coca
  of Father Buinaima.   55
At once,
  blown with that breath,
  the Father's heart
  becomes sweet,
  becomes cool.   60
From then on
  the Father's name is
  Cool Tobacco,
  Sweet Coca.
In this way it concludes.   65

"SEEKING OUT THE GARDEN WORK"
"INVOCATION FOR THE PREGNANT MOTHER"

The Word of life forms itself as Things—food, game, offspring. This formation takes place through work. It is this work that the words of text 2 are seeking.

The previous text was about the seed of that Word of life. In this text Kinerai shows that that seed is "breath" *(jagiyi)*. To make that seed sprout one has to deposit it in the womb of the Mother. This Mother "is Working Mother" (line 3).

"Working Mother" is my rendering of the Uitoto term *jieño,* contraction of the expression *jiérede eiño. Eiño* means "mother"; *jiérede* means "to be a hard worker/hunter," and derives from the root *jie-* which means "hunting," in a broad sense. One could thus translate the word *jieño* as "Working Mother" or as "Hunting Mother." The Mother's "hunting" is the work on the cultivated plants. Kinerai explains:

> The tobacco spirit is breath, it does not have the spirit of animals
> . . . The hunting of tobacco is the hunting of all animals and is the
> work of the garden plants. When one prepares tobacco paste and
> names an animal, that animal falls there. That is tobacco hunting.
> When one wants to go hunting one mixes tobacco paste [with
> vegetable salt], names the animal, and it falls.

When he says "to name an animal" it has to be understood that, when preparing and mixing tobacco paste, animals are not named by their proper names but in an indirect fashion, "because the animals listen and get scared away." This is particularly true in the Word of dancing rituals when tobacco paste is mixed and distributed to the people so that they can get game. There, animals are named as "breath" of fruit trees and cultivated and wild plants, in much the same way as Kinerai does here. So, for instance, "breath of green *umari"* means tapir, "breath of black *umari"* means collared peccary, "breath of *cumare* palm" means white-lipped peccary, "breath of *juansoco"* means woolly monkey, and so forth.[1]

The ancient people discovered these sets of relations, Kinerai says, by means of "tobacco drunkenness and dreams." This can be appreciated in detail in text 2B, "The Dreams of Abundance," which follows, together with a commentary.

The wild animals and the plants of the garden are identical in the Mother's womb. Text 1 spoke about "the seed"; now this seed has filled the Mother's womb. The Word, in form of breath (intention) enters the Mother (the tangible world) and makes her pregnant.

The undifferentiated breath begins to take shape through the names. In the

Recently planted food-plot

third verse (lines 8-26) Kínerai recites the names of many crops. This unique breath starts to differentiate itself into specific cultivated plants. He recites, in the whole text, the names of 20 plants, corresponding to 17 botanical species and some varieties of these species (see appendix 1 for the botanical classification of all the mentioned plants). These are the main traditional cultivated crops "on the woman's part." Note that tobacco and coca, two prominent plants, are not mentioned—these are crops "on the man's part."

For this breath to turn into proper plants it is not enough just to name their names, it is also necessary to work. This work starts with clearing of the lowest tier of the mature forest, then goes on to the slashing of the trees, and, when they are dry, to the burning of the whole plot. This is what is called slash and burn agriculture. He refers succinctly to this set of activities when he says (lines 27-32):

Later on, further ahead,
   —truly—
   after having
   resolved to work,
   one already has
   a slashed jungle clearing
There, the seeds will be planted.

47

Mature food-plot with manioc plants

In the second and third stanzas, he recites how the different plants are harvested and how these plants take existence. "Everything is harvested," he concludes (line 61).

This is not merely an explanation of the process by which plants take form out of the tobacco breath in the Mother's womb. This recitation is a healing spell to cure the Working Mother's womb and ensure that the garden work is successfully completed.

The breath in the Mother's womb is like an illness, literally a "flatulence" *(zegore)*—see stanza 4 (lines 62-69). The Word of *rafue* enters the Mother (the world) and upsets her. If one leaves that Word aside and does not work to harvest it, the Mother weakens and the Word takes the form of an illness. But when that Word is harvested in the form of plants, the Mother is relieved. For this reason, the Word to seek out the garden work is also a healing spell to conjure the Mother.

In the same fourth stanza he says: "That is the very origin of our life" (line 65). The Mother gets ill with the breath of the cultivated plants; likewise a woman, when she is fertilized by a man, "gets drunk with the breath of tobacco" (text 2A, lines 5-6). From this, a healing spell for pregnant women was obtained (see text 2A).

When read together, the texts explain each other. Text 2A explains how the mother gets ill with the breath of fire of the father, text 2 explains how the Mother

48

"Considering that there is food thus those things appeared"

gets relieved of that flatulence through the word that propitiates the growth of plants.

Both texts are healing spells to cure the feminine body. None of them is an actual spell, they are only "the word" *(úai)* of the spell. The text of the actual spell contains the same elements of the word but they are recited in the form of a chant. The spell is not recited aloud, only its melody is whistled. That is why the subtitle to text 2A reads "only the word," and by the end of text 2 it also reads "it was already proved as a good Word / —only the word" (lines 92-93).

Part II of text 2 refers to the appearance of baskets and other woven tools necessary to harvest and process foodstuffs. The set of objects spoken about here are snares to trap the stuff that just came out of the Mother's womb. For both gardening and trap-hunting woven tools are used. The Working Mother is also Hunting Mother, game is like cultivated food. Thus food, both vegetable and animal, has to be snared in this basketry.

The woven basket is a powerful metaphor. The basket, Kɨneraɨ says, is a person. A tradition of rituals is also called a basket, and the master of those rituals is called "the basket holder." When a person completes a training (as healer or master of rituals), it is said that he/she "closed his/her basket." The places where ancient people lived are also referred to as baskets, and if a person wants to live

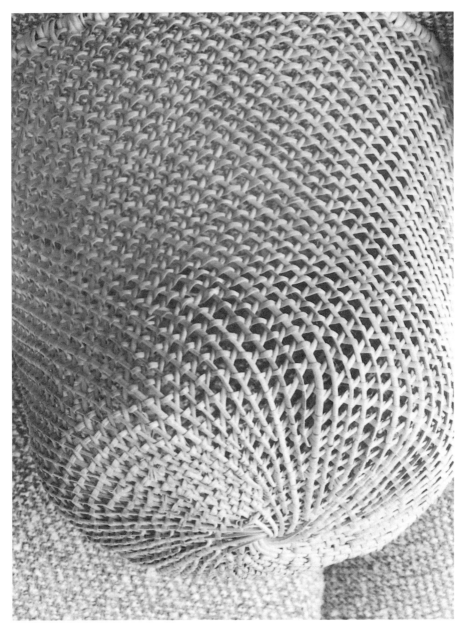

in those places he/she has to know the Word of that basket. The texts presented in this volume are from Kinerai's basket. And this book is a new basket that holds them together.

Baskets are made with threads of vines. The thread *(igai)* stands for "thought." The thread is what holds us to the Mother, the umbilical cord, the thread of life.

When a sorcerer or a powerful person travels with his/her thought it is said that he/she is travelling "in the thread of dream." A material basket is a woven thread, likewise a person is a woven thread of dream.

The appearance of basketry introduces a new element in the development of *rafue*. Men make baskets and other woven devices for women to work with. Basketry symbolizes exogamy and marriage alliances. These alliances are going to hold new life—children. Text 2 is the basis that allows the development of the Word of the next text, the Word of discipline for young people. That is why he says, in lines 80-81: "But out of nothing / there is nothing to tell." The Word of food (text 2) has to be complete before proceeding into marriage, children, and education. These baskets—woven threads, alliances—hold the breath from the Mother's womb in the threads of dreams.

Monifue nɨkaɨ

Monifue nɨkaɨ mei
  táɨniano.
Mei nano fueñe ua
  dɨona fɨnódɨmɨe,   *jm*
  jíibina fɨnódɨmɨe,   *jm* jm   5
  nano fueñe mei dɨona nɨkaɨ fɨnode,   *jm* jm
  ua aiyo naɨraɨ komuiya nɨkaɨ,   *jm*
  aiyo jíibina komuiya nɨkaɨ.   *jm* jm
Naɨ
  afe fakaize mei iñede,   10
  naɨ nɨkaɨ ua monifue nɨkaɨna onóiñede.   *jm* jm

Ie jira ua
  nɨkáɨrite,   *jm* jm
  dɨona fɨnódɨmɨe nɨkáɨriya.   *jm*
Nɨkáɨrite   15
  ua dɨona ua nɨnomo aiyo ua komuide,   *jm* jm
  jíibina ua aiyo ua komúiyena nɨkáɨrite.   *jm* jm
Ie jira ua, nɨnomo ite, ua
  ua ite dɨónana kɨódɨkue,   *jm*
  nɨnomo ite jíibinana kɨódɨkue.   *jm* jm   20

Ie jira ua nabéfuena
  ua dɨónari jɨfaide.   *jm* jm
Jɨfaide ua,
  ja akɨ dɨnómona
  ja ua dɨónana ua kɨode.   *jm* jm   25
Daade ua ijɨmona
  ja ua aiyo komuide,   *jm* jm
  jae fia ie kɨona.   *jm* jɨɨ
Ie mei ua dano ja,
  ja mel fjɨɨɨo   30

The Dreams of Abundance

[I]

The dreams of abundance
  start here.
At the beginning
  the maker of tobacco,
  the maker of coca,   5
  at the beginning had a dream of tobacco,
  a dream of many people growing,
  a dream of many coca plants growing.
Still
  at that moment, it was not,   10
  still the dreams of abundance were unknown.

Then truly
  he dreamt,
  the maker of tobacco had dreams.
He dreamt   15
  that a great many plants of tobacco grew,
  he dreamt that many plants of coca were growing.
Then truly, [he thought] "Where is it?
  Where is the tobacco I saw?
  Where is the coca I saw?"   20

Then truly,
  he resolutely got drunk with tobacco.
He got drunk,
  and from then on
  now he truly saw the tobacco.   25
From a single seed
  many were now growing—
  those which, before, he had only seen.
Then, truly, again,
  from that seed   30

íjɨmona ja ua kɨode aiyo ua dɨona komúiyena.   *jm* jm
Daaje izoi jíibina
   nano fueñe ua daa kɨode ua iémona aiyo jíibinana ja komuide.   *jm* jm

Ie baɨmo ua
   ja ɨkobe úrue ua komuiye ua izoi,   35
   afe nɨkaɨna kɨode.   *jm* jm
Ie izoi eróikana
   ite afeno.   *jm* jm
Meita ja ua
   naɨraɨ dánomo ua   40
   ja komuiya ua
   ie ua jiyakɨ.   *jm* jm

                                                  [II]

Iémona
   afe izoi eróikana
   dano ua afe dɨona jagɨyɨdo ua,   45
   jíibina jagɨyɨdo,
   ja dano nɨkaɨrite.   *jm* jm
Ja ua akɨ dɨnómona monifue nɨkaɨ   *jm* jm
   idɨ monífuena kɨode.   *jm* jm
Ie jira ua,   50
   ua rozídoro komuiya nɨkaɨ,   *jm* jm
   ja akɨ dɨnómona
   ja ua,
   ua nomedo komuiya nɨkaɨ,   *jm* jm
   mazaka nɨkaɨ,   *jm*   55
   beyado nɨkaɨ,   *jm* jm
   ua júe áidua nɨkaɨ,   *jm* jm
   mɨzeyɨ guiya nɨkaɨ,   *jm* jm
   jizaiño rɨia nɨkaɨ,   *jm* jm
   jɨrɨkue rɨia nɨkaɨ,   *jm* jm   60
   konónue rɨia nɨkaɨ,   *jm* jm
   ua kɨnekɨ kaɨa nɨkaɨ,   *jm* jm
   ua bene monifue ua
   nekazɨ kaɨa nɨkaɨ,   *jm* jɨɨ
   nemozɨ kaɨa nɨkaɨ,   *jm* jm   65

he had seen, from that seed many tobacco plants would grow.
Likewise the coca,
   first he saw a single one, and from that many had grown.

And further on
   then children will grow,   35
   as he saw in that dream.
And so
   it is.
And thus, truly,
   is the origin   40
   of the rebirth
   of the people.

                                               [II]
From then on
   in the same way,
   again, truly, with breath of tobacco,   45
   and with breath of coca,
   he dreamt again.
From that moment on he dreamt of abundance,
   and he saw what is true abundance.
Then, truly,   50
   the dream of the pineapple's growth,
   from then on,
   truly,
   the dream of the avocado's growth,
   the dream of peanut,   55
   the dream of maize,
   the dream of digging up manioc tubers,
   the dream of eating cacao seeds,
   the dream of sucking fruits of inga,
   the dream of sucking forest grapes,   60
   the dream of sucking sugar cane,
   the dream of gnawing fruits of miriti palm,
   —this is true abundance—
   the dream of gnawing fruits of green *umari,*
   the dream of gnawing fruits of yellow *umari,*   65

goido kaɨa nɨkaɨ,   *jm*
obedo kaɨa nɨkaɨ,   *jm* jm
uibijɨ guiya nɨkaɨ;   *jm* jm
monifue nɨkaɨ.   *jm* jm

Ie izoi eróikana   70
  roziyɨ rɨia nɨkaɨ fɨnódɨkue, ja daɨde,   *jm* jɨɨ
  meita ofómana monaide.   *jm* jm
Nomedo kue rɨia nɨkaɨ daɨde,
  ja ua ja nɨmaido monaide.   *jm* jm
Mɨzeyɨ rɨia nɨkaɨ,   75
  ɨmena monaide.   *jm* jm jm
Jizaiño rɨia nɨkaɨ,
  kuitana monaide.   *jm*
Jɨrɨkue rɨia nɨkaɨ,
  áikɨna monaide.   *jm* jm   80
Kɨnekɨ kaɨana nɨkaɨ,   *jm*
  ɨmena monaide.   *jm* jm
Uibijɨ guiya nɨkaɨ,
  jɨkona monaide.   *jm* jm
Ifákɨe guiya nɨkaɨ,   85
  jɨko ɨfokɨ.   *jm* jm
Júe áiduana nɨkáɨritɨkue,   *jm* jm
  aiyo chamu oye nɨkaɨ fɨnode.   *jm* jm
Mazaka guiya nɨkaɨ,   *jm*
  ñenɨgo ie fayena.   *jm* jm   90
Kirɨgaɨna nɨkáɨritɨkue,   *jm* jm
  jɨko nɨkaɨ.   *jm* jm
Zibe nɨkaɨ,   *jm* jm
  zurúyari nɨkaɨ.   *jm* jm
Akie izóikana   95
  ite monifue nɨkaɨ.   *jm*
Konónue rɨia nɨkaɨ,
  jemɨ rɨye nɨkaɨ.   *jm* jm
Akɨ dɨnómona ja arɨ
  nɨkaɨ, monifue nɨkaɨ monaide,   *jm* jm   100
  dɨnomo ñenɨgaɨ ja ua monaide.   *jm* jm

the dream of gnawing fruits of black *umari goido,*
the dream of gnawing fruits of black *umari obedo,*
the dream of eating breadfruits;
dreams of abundance.

In the same way,   70
    I had a dream of sucking pineapple, one says,
    and so, the day dawns with great tinamou.
I dreamt of eating avocado, one says,
    now, truly, the day dawns with coati.
A dream of eating fruits of cacao,   75
    the day dawns with paca.
A dream of sucking fruits of inga,
    the day dawns with kinkajou.
A dream of sucking forest grapes,
    the day dawns with titi monkey.   80
A dream of gnawing miriti palm fruits,
    the day dawns with paca.
A dream of eating breadfruits,
    the day dawns with jaguar.
A dream of eating brazil nuts   85
    is a jaguar's head.
I dreamt of digging up manioc tubers,
    it is a dream of catching many fish.
A dream of eating peanuts
    is to kill small armadillo.   90
I dreamt of a basket,
    it is a dream of giant armadillo.
A dream of a clay griddle
    is a dream of black jaguar.
Such are   95
    the dreams of abundance.
A dream of sucking sugar cane
    is a dream of eating woolly monkey.
From then on
    the dreams of abundance dawned,   100
    and there the armadillo basket dawns.[1]

Jíibie duana nɨkáɨritɨkue,   *jm* jm
  yaiño fayena.   *jm* jm
Rabɨna nɨkáɨritɨkue,   *jm*
  doboyi nɨkaɨ.   *jm* jm   105
Jiménana nɨkáɨritɨkue,
  jimekɨ guiyana,   *jm*
  jadie zeema nɨ́kaɨ,   *jm*
  zeema rɨyɨkaɨ.   *jm* jm
Toguéyɨna nɨkáɨritɨkue,   110
  kuita rɨye nɨkaɨ.   *jm* jm   jm
Akie izoi
  monifue nɨkaɨ ja monaide.   *jm* jm jm

Dunajɨ guiyana nɨkáɨritɨkue,   *jm* jm
  zuruma éɨdiri nɨkaɨ.   *jm* jm   115
Jakaie guiya nɨkaɨ, daɨde,   *jm*
  jadie fɨénide nɨkaɨ daɨde,   *jm*
  roiye nɨkaɨ daɨde.   *jm* jm   jm
Kɨ́ifo mia nɨkaɨ,   *jm*
  jadie o bofédaiye nɨkaɨ daɨde.   *jm* jm   120
Yomejɨ guiya nɨkaɨ,   *jm*
  jadie okaina eroiko o rɨye nɨkaɨ daɨde.   *jm* jm

                                                            [III]
Akie izoi eróikano monifue nɨkaɨ,
  ja ua jíibina fɨnódɨmɨe, dɨona fɨnódɨmɨe
  nɨkáɨriya nɨkaɨna kaɨmo úrite.   *jm* jɨɨ   125
Meita monífuena nɨkáɨriadɨ
  jadie ñuera nɨkaɨ daɨde.   *jm* jm
Meita ja ua ɨnɨakania,
  ja ua jíibina fɨnode urukɨ ja ɨnɨakade,   *jm* jm
  jirari ua ñuera nɨkaɨna kue yóitɨo, daɨde,   *jm* jm   130
  jíibina komuiya nɨkaɨ,
  dɨona komuiya nɨkaɨ daɨde,   *jm* jɨɨ
  farékatofe komuiya nɨkaɨ daɨde,   *jm* jɨɨ
  mazákarɨ komuiya nɨkaɨ daɨde,   *jm* jm
  íɨna kue yóitɨo daɨde,   *jm* jm   135

I dreamt of *mambeing* coca,
  it is to kill a three-toed sloth.
I dreamt of chili paste,
  it is a dream of tamandua.   105
I dreamt of peach palm
  —eating peach palm fruits,
  it is a dream of speckled cayman
  —a dream of eating cayman.
I dreamt of *anon* fruit,   110
  it is a dream of eating kinkajou.
In this way
  the dreams of abundance dawn.

I dreamt of eating cocoyam tubers,
  it is a dream of tapir's hoofs.   115
A dream of eating yam
  means it is a bad dream,
  it is a dream of breaking a bone.
A dream of licking honey
  means you will suffer an injury.   120
A dream of eating cassava cakes,[2]
  that dream means that you will eat animal's flank.

                                                  [III]
Thus are the dreams of abundance,
  now truly, as the coca maker, as the tobacco maker dreamt,
  so our dreams speak to us.   125
And so, if one dreams of abundance,
  that means it is a good dream.
And so, when one wants to sleep,
  when the people who prepare coca want to sleep,
  then, "You have to send me good dreams," they say,   130
  "the dream of coca's growth,
  the dream of tobacco's growth," they say,
  "the dream of sweet manioc's growth," they say,
  "the dream of peanut's growth," they say,
  "those you have to send me," they say,   135

monifue nɨkaɨna kue nɨkáɨriyena.   *jm* jm
Ja ua jíibie dute
  urukɨ ja ɨnɨakaniadɨ
  akɨ daɨi ja ua
  éikome akɨ daɨi ja jɨkade.   *jm* jm   140

Meita ja ɨnɨde urukɨ ja ua
  monifue nɨkaɨna nɨkáɨrite,   *jm* jm
  monifue igaɨ, monifue kɨrɨtikoɨ,
  akɨ dɨnori ja monaide.   *jm* jm
Nɨɨ mei ua   145
  jíibina dɨona fɨnode ua
  jɨfaiya diónado akɨ monifue nɨkaɨna
  monáitakana uite.   *jm* jɨɨ
Meita ie yezika
  mei nɨno fɨénide nɨkaɨna iñede,   *jm* jɨɨ   150
  rofokɨ nɨkaɨna iñede,   *jm*
  faiyékɨaɨ nɨkaɨna iñede,
  nana monifue nɨkaɨ.   *jm* jɨɨ

Jino jazíkɨmo ua
  ñekɨkɨ kaɨ guiyana nɨkaɨ eimoɨ o fayena daɨde.   *jm* jm   155
Bene ua,
  jíibiyuna bɨɨide,   *jm*
  ie nɨkaɨ fɨnódɨkue,   *jm*
  jadie mɨgui o rɨyena,
  jíibiyuna kɨódɨo daɨde.   *jm* jm   160
Baie ifákɨdona nɨkáɨriadɨ,
  baie mei janáyari ɨfokɨ daɨde.   *jm* jm

Ie ja,
  ja ɨnɨde mei akie ɨnɨaɨkɨ
  ñuera ɨnɨaɨkɨ   165
  mei jɨfáɨdɨmɨe kakana.   *jm* jm
Nɨɨ ua nanoide ua monífuena nɨkaɨ,
  ie mei bie ua riároɨkɨ mamékɨdo mei
  nana ua nanoide monifue mamekɨ ite.   *jm* jm

60

"so that I can have dreams of abundance."
Now truly, when the people
  who *mambe* coca want to sleep,
  in that way, truly,
  in that way the old man asks.   140

And so, the people who sleep
  have dreams of abundance—
  the thread of abundance, the basket of abundance,
  up to that point it dawns.
Likewise, truly,   145
  he who prepares tobacco and coca
  keeps making those dreams of abundance dawn
  in the tobacco drunkenness.
And so, in that moment,
  then there are no bad dreams,   150
  there are no ominous dreams,
  there are no dreams of misfortune,
  all are dreams of abundance.

Out there in the forest, the dream
  of eating *cumare* fruits means one will kill white-lipped peccary. 155
On the other hand,
  I had a dream of
  a bag of *mambe* lying there;
  then you will eat small agouti,
  you saw a bag of *mambe,* one says.   160
If one dreams of a seed of brazil nuts
  that means a jaguar's head.

And now
  when they sleep, their sleep
  is a good sleep   165
  because the one who gets drunk with tobacco is paying attention.
These are the dreams of abundance of the beginnings,
  and then with the names of those plants of today
  there are names for all the abundance of the beginnings.

Ie mei ua 170
  aiyo farékare komúiyana nɨkáɨriadɨ
  mei rɨgóniaɨ ua rɨgózaɨaɨ komuiya. *jm* jɨɨ
Mei ua jíibinana nɨkáɨnia ua
  aiyo urúiaɨ komuide, *jm* jm
  daaje izoi dɨona. *jm* jm jm 175

Meita akɨ dɨnomo
  ja ua arɨ
  ja mei ua nɨkaɨna itɨno ja ua monaide,
  ie mei batɨno nanoide monifue ja monaide. *jm* jm
Akɨ dɨno 180
  arɨ mei monáiyanona
  itɨno mei
  ja ua
  ja arɨ ua monaide, mei ja baie ua afeno ja mei ua
  kaɨ kɨona. *jm* jm jm 185
Akie izoide *jm* jm
  ñúefuena ua fuite. *jm* jm

COMMENTARY ON TEXT 2B:

"THE DREAMS OF ABUNDANCE"

This text deals with the "true" dreams, dreams of food and people's growth. In this way the maker of tobacco and coca asks to dream when he goes to sleep (see lines 123-140). Other dreams—ominous dreams—are not spoken of here: those have their origin in another story.[1] The dreams of abundance have their origin in the Working Mother, who is also the Hunting Mother. That is why the metaphors that rule these dreams are the cultivated crops of the garden.

  Those metaphors are very old and they are common to the Uitoto and several neighboring cultures. Kɨneraɨ says that the ancients discovered those relations by means of tobacco intoxication. When the tree of *Moniya Amena*—"The Tree of Abundance" that could bear all fruits and cultivated plants—fell to earth, according to the myth, all those fruits sunk into the water (literally sunk into *rɨbei*,

And then   170
   if one dreams of many plants of sweet manioc growing,
   many women and girls will be born.
And if one dream of coca plants
   many boys will be born,
   the same [if one dreams of] tobacco plants.   175

And so, at that point,
   truly,
   all that is dreamt has already dawned,
   and beyond that, the abundance of the beginnings dawned.
At that point,   180
   all that was
   about to dawn,
   truly,
   has already dawned, and there
   we saw it.   185
In this way
   the good Word concludes.

---

the mother's amniotic fluid).[2] Those primordial "fruits"—"abundance of the beginnings"—were brought back into the world by the ancients by means of dreams and tobacco intoxication, and in that way they became today's crops.

That abundance of the beginning is also the root of people's growth, and the root of the forest's wild game. The first dream of the maker of tobacco and coca is of these two plants, a dream of many people who will be born. Those two plants, together with sweet manioc, are the representation of men and women (see lines 170-175). To make that dream become truth, the maker of tobacco and coca has to walk the whole path of *rafue:* Word of food, Word of baskets, Word of discipline, Word of healing, Word of dancing rituals. Then he will see a lot of people; at the beginning he saw just one seed. Part I of the text deals with this dream; here, Kɨneraɨ refers to his own biography (see third fragment by Kɨneraɨ in this book's Introduction).

The animals of the forest are also the abundance of the beginnings (fruits of the Tree of Abundance). These animals are "the pineapple," "the peach palm," "the sapote," and so forth, of the jaguar, the ocelot, the anaconda, the harpy eagle, and the other masters of the forest. The former animals are the latter's "fruits" (game). But all of them are tobacco and coca's game, that is, people's game. That is why, when preparing and mixing tobacco, the forest game are given the names of today's plants and fruits (see lines 167-169). Likewise, in dreams, those animals appear in the form of those fruits and plants.

Part II of the text and two stanzas of part III deal with the meaning of those dreams. The following notes contain a summary of those meanings, in the same order in which they appear in the text, along with some additional commentaries provided by Kɨnerai and other people. Biological identification of all plants and animals mentioned can be found in the appendices.[3]

(Numbers in parentheses refer to the lines of the text)

A DREAM OF SUCKING PINEAPPLE: THE DAY DAWNS WITH GREAT TINAMOU. (70-72) The great tinamou's wing resembles the external form of a pineapple.

A DREAM OF EATING AVOCADO: THE DAY DAWNS WITH COATI. (73-74) The elongated form of the avocado resembles a coati's head.

A DREAM OF EATING FRUITS OF CACAO: THE DAY DAWNS WITH PACA. (75-76) The longitudinal lines of the fruit of cacao resemble the lateral lines on the paca's body.

A DREAM OF SUCKING FRUITS OF INGA: THE DAY DAWNS WITH KINKAJOU. (77-78) The kinkajou eats the fruits of inga when they are in season, during the rainy months of April and May.

A DREAM OF SUCKING FOREST GRAPES: THE DAY DAWNS WITH TITI MONKEY. (79-80) The forest grape, when it is ripe, is black like the titi monkey's fur; also, that fruit is part of its diet.

A DREAM OF GNAWING MIRITI PALM FRUITS: THE DAY DAWNS WITH PACA. (81-82) The paca's fur is reddish like the miriti palm fruit; also, this fruit is part of its diet.

A DREAM OF EATING BREADFRUITS: THE DAY DAWNS WITH JAGUAR. (83-84) The breadfruit has "knots" that give it the appearance of a jaguar's paw. In the Caquetá river region, this fruit is also called jaguar's paw.

A DREAM OF EATING BRAZIL NUTS: THE DAY DAWNS WITH A JAGUAR'S HEAD. (85-86, 161-162) The fruit of brazil nuts is big, like a jaguar's head and its seeds are white and long like this animal's canine teeth.

A DREAM OF DIGGING UP MANIOC TUBERS: THE DAY DAWNS WITH MANY FISH. (87-88) In the myth of the Tree of Abundance the manioc tubers that fell into the water turned into fish.

A DREAM OF EATING PEANUTS: THE DAY DAWNS WITH SMALL ARMADILLO. (89-90) The shell of the peanut is grooved, resembling the small armadillo's transversal skin plates. In addition, a type of basket called "small armadillo's" *(ñenigai)* is used to store peanuts (see also text 3A).

A DREAM OF A BASKET: THE DAY DAWNS WITH GIANT ARMADILLO. (91-92) In text 3B a dream of a big basket is interpreted as the hunting of a giant armadillo (see lines 96-107, text 3B). In text 3A the open-weave basket is presented as "the portrait" of the giant armadillo. In the present text, Kɨnerai uses the expression *jɨko* which is generic for all felines and also includes domestic dogs. According to Dolores Yaci and Juan de la Cruz Hichamón, Uitoto-Murui Indians of the Caraparaná river, the giant armadillo is also called *jɨkobainaño* (information of Diego L. Muñoz and Ma. del Pilar Rivas), which leads us to believe that the expression *jɨko* does not refer to a feline but, in abbreviated form, to a giant armadillo.

A DREAM OF A CLAY GRIDDLE: THE DAY DAWNS WITH BLACK JAGUAR. (93-94) The black jaguar's fur resembles the bottom of a clay griddle, which becomes black with use.

A DREAM OF SUCKING SUGAR CANE: THE DAY DAWNS WITH WOOLLY MONKEY. (97-98) The tail of a woolly monkey, when it has been cooked, resembles the stem of sugar cane. In addition, according to the myth of the origin of the tribes, when the first human beings came out of the hole of origin, they had tails, which the hero Buinaima cut off; those tails turned into stems of sugar cane.

A DREAM OF MAMBEING COCA: THE DAY DAWNS WITH THREE-TOED SLOTH. (102-103) The basic diet of the sloth consists of leaves of trees; it is said that those leaves are its coca.

A DREAM OF CHILI PASTE: THE DAY DAWNS WITH TAMANDUA. (104-105) In the tamandua story, his father-in-law punishes him for being lazy and drowsy by pushing his snout into a chili paste. That is why the tip of the tamandua's snout is dark.

A DREAM OF EATING PEACH PALM FRUITS: THE DAY DAWNS WITH SPECKLED CAYMAN. (106-109) The speckled cayman's eye looks red at night, like a peach palm fruit. In addition, according to the myth of the origin of the peach palm, in former times it belonged to the aquatic beings.

A DREAM OF *ANON:* THE DAY DAWNS WITH KINKAJOU. (110-111) It is said that the grease of the kinkajou, when it is fat, resembles the white pulp of *anon*.

A DREAM OF EATING COCOYAM TUBERS: THE DAY DAWNS WITH TAPIR'S HOOFS. (114-115) The cocoyam tubers are small and their shape resembles a tapir's hoof.

A DREAM OF EATING YAM: THE DAY DAWNS WITH A BONE FRACTURE.[4] (116-118) The swelling produced by a bone fracture resembles the round shape of yam, which also has a reddish color.

A DREAM OF LICKING HONEY: THE DAY DAWNS WITH AN INJURY. (119-120) It is said that bee honey is people's blood and that children should never have it uncooked.

A DREAM OF EATING CASSAVA CAKES: THE DAY DAWNS WITH AN ANIMAL'S FLANK. (121-122) An animal's flank is thick, like the cassava cakes (which are thicker and softer than the cassava bread—see note 2 to text 2B).

A DREAM OF EATING *CUMARE* PALM FRUITS: THE DAY DAWNS WITH WHITE-LIPPED PECCARY. (154-155) White-lipped peccaries eat *cumare* palm fruits when they are in season, from July to September.

A DREAM OF A BAG OF *MAMBE:* THE DAY DAWNS WITH SMALL AGOUTI. (156-160) It is said that the small agouti's fur is like the waste parts of coca leaves after they have been toasted, pounded, and strained.

A DREAM OF PLANTS OF SWEET MANIOC: THE DAY DAWNS WITH WOMEN AND GIRLS. (170-172) Young women are called *farékatofe,* "stem of sweet manioc."

A DREAM OF PLANTS OF TOBACCO AND COCA: THE DAY DAWNS WITH MEN. (173-175) It is said that a man's tongue is a tobacco leaf, and his Adam's apple is a *yeraki* (tobacco paste recipient).

(See explanation of the Tree of Dreams on the following two pages)

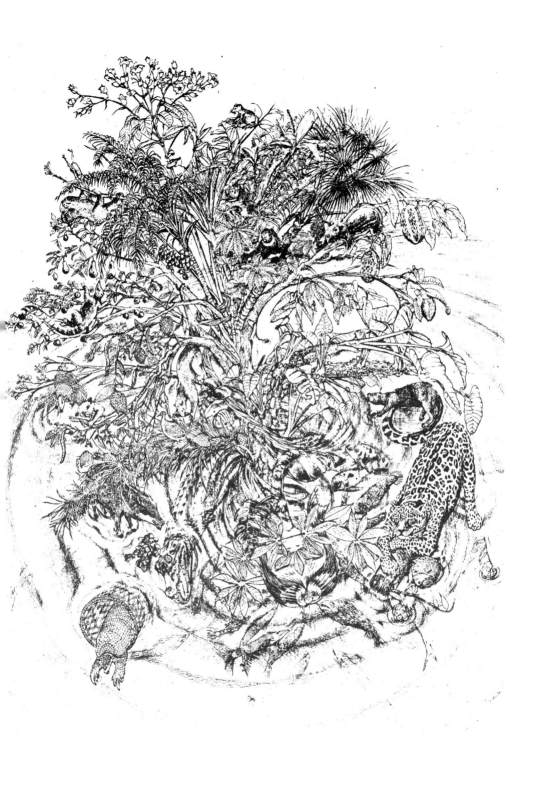

Animals and People in the Tree of Dreams

1 Woman	7 White-lipped peccary	14 Paca
2 Fish	8 Great tinamou	15 Titi monkey
3 Jaguar	9 Tapir	16 Woolly monkey
4 Black jaguar	10 Tamandua	17 Three-toed sloth
5 Giant armadillo	11 Kinkajou	18 Small agouti
6 Speckled cayman	12 Small armadillo	19 Man
	13 Coati	

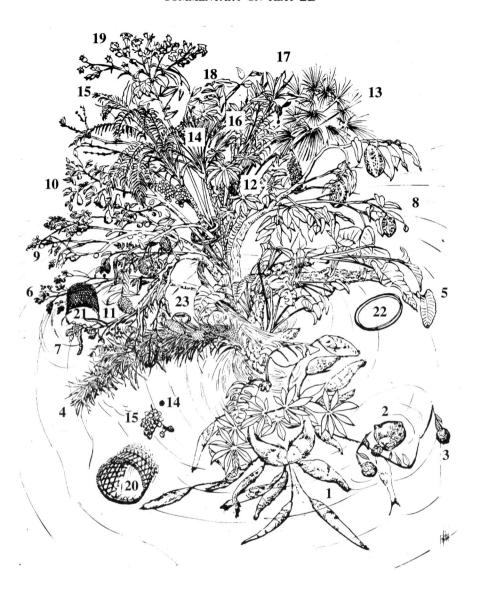

Plants and Objects in the Tree of Dreams

1 Manioc tubers	9 Sapote	17 Plantain
2 Brazil nut	10 Avocado	18 Coca
3 Breadfruit	11 *Anon*	19 Tobacco
4 Pineapple	12 Forest grape	20 Opean-weave basket
5 Cocoyam	13 Miriti palm	21 Narrow-weave basket
6 Peanut	14 *Cumare* palm	22 Clay griddle
7 Inga	15 Peach palm	23 Chili pot
8 Cacao	16 Sugar cane	

69

THE FATHER'S LEAF

Bibe 3
Yetárafue

Mei ua moo nɨbena uaina ite,   *jm* jm
  ua jae mei eiño ie kaɨ yoga.   *jm* jm
Moo íena itɨno ua
  mei ja dɨnomo ja moo
  komekɨ úriyafue   *jm* jm   5
  ñuéfuena itɨno   *jm* jm *jm* jm
  bie úrue komúiyena,   *jm* jm
  bie rɨgoza komúiyena.   *jm* jm

O mirɨgo,   *jm*
  o ɨio   *jm*   10
  daɨnano.   *jm* jm *jm*
Ja nɨɨ abɨna
  onóikana jáaiyena.   *jm* jm

Bie o ɨɨ (daɨde),   *jm* jm
  ɨɨ   *jm*   15
    jiza o mirɨgo (daɨde),   *jm* jm
  ɨɨ jiza rɨgózaniadɨ o ebuño (daɨde).   *jm* jm
Abɨna ónoitɨoza,   *jm* jm
  ebena úriñeitɨoza.   *jm* jm
Ja mei raiyano.   *jm* jm *jm* jm   20

Izo jito   *jm*
  o aama (daɨde),   *jm* jm
  izo jiza o mirɨgo.   *jm* jm
Akie izóikana ja
  ua yokana uiga.   *jm* jm   25
Ie úrue abɨna mei onode,   *jm*
   rɨgoza,   *jm*
    ɨiza (daɨde)   *jm*
  abɨna onode.   *jm* jm *jm*

Text 3
The Word on Discipline

[I]

These are the words of the Father's Leaf;
  the Mother's we already told.
What belongs to the Father—
  then, in that point,
  the talk of the Father's heart   5
  are good teachings
  for this boy to grow up with,
  for this girl to grow up with.

Boy, this is your sister,[1]
  girl, this is your brother,[2]   10
  one says.
So that they start
  learning how to behave.

This is your aunt (one says),
  the daughter   15
    of the aunt is the boy's sister (one says),
  the daughter of the aunt is the girl's sister (one says).
You must know how to behave,
  you mustn't say naughty things.
So one says.   20

The son of the paternal uncle
  is the boy's brother (one says),
  the daughter of the paternal uncle is the boy's sister.
In this manner
  one keeps teaching them.   25
And that child knows how to behave,
    the girl
    and the boy
  know how to behave with one another.

73

Oni bie o uzuǥo (daɨde),   *jm* jm   30
   mamékɨñeitɨoza.   *jm* jm
Oni o uzuma (daɨde),   *jm* jm
   féekuizo uzu ráitɨoza.   *jm* jm
Oni o biyama (daɨde),   *jm* jm
   biyama ráitɨoza,   *jm* jm   35
   mamékɨñeitɨoza.   *jm*

Eikome abɨ fáɨgataiza   *jm*
   yokano atɨka.   *jm* jm
Ebena ñáɨñeitɨoza (daɨde),   *jm* jm *jm* jm
   zairide jitaɨǥo ebena ñáɨñeitɨo,   *jm*   40
   zairide jitókome ebena ñáɨñeitɨo.   *jm* jm
Abɨ úiñoyena   *jm*
   yoga.   *jm* jm jm *jm*

                                                  [II][i]
Ie jira dɨnómona   *jm*
   bie izoide (daɨde).   *jm* jm   45
Zairide jitókome (daɨde)   *jm* jm
   abɨna onoiri.   *jm* [cough] *jm* jm
Zairide jitaɨǥo daɨde   *jm*
   abɨna onoiri.   *jm* jm jm *jm*

Zairide jitókome ja   50
   gakue ote.   *jm*
Oni, kɨrɨtikoɨ nítɨoza (daɨde),   *jm* jm
   kɨrigaɨ nítɨoza (daɨde),   *jm* jm
   ranita nítɨoza (daɨde),   *jm*
   yokofe nítɨoza (daɨde).   *jm*   55

Rɨǥoza dɨbene
   jaɨnoibi óitɨoza,   *jm* jm
   taɨkadu táitɨoza   *jm*
     jifirai riyena,   *jm* jm
     mazákarɨ riyena,   *jm* jm   60
     farékatofe jɨyena.   *jm* jm jm jm *jm*

Furthermore, this is your grandmother (one says),   30
  you won't call her by her name.
Furthermore, your grandfather (one says),
  gently, you will call him "grandfather."
Furthermore, your maternal uncle (one says),
  you will call him "uncle,"   35
  you won't call him by his name.

So as not to upset the elders,
  one keeps teaching them.
You won't say naughty things (one says),
  a girl who is growing up shouldn't speak unproperly,   40
  a boy who is growing up shouldn't speak unproperly.
They are taught
  to take care of themselves.

                                                [II][i]
From then on,
  it is like this (one says).   45
The boy who grows up
  must behave himself.
The girl who grows up, one says,
  must behave herself.

The boy who grows up   50
  opens a food-plot in an abandoned jungle clearing.
Furthermore, you will weave a small basket (one says),
  you will weave a basket (one says),
  you will weave a manioc sieve (one says),
  you will weave a manioc strainer (one says).   55

On the girl's part
  you will fetch water,
  you will dig up a piece of land
    to sow chili,
    to sow peanut,   60
    to plant sweet manioc.

Ebena ñáiñeitioza,   *jm* jm
 dunayi rítioza.   *jm* jm
Nine kai jebegoi túuiñede,   *jm* jm
 jiaima ie jétai dainaza   *jm* jm   65
 yoga.   *jm* jm jm *jm*
Jamáiruiñeitioza.   *jm* jm
Ie rigoza, ja ua, tíiriyana onode,   *jm* jii
 raa jetájana onode.   *jm* jm jm *jm* jii *jm*

                                                      [ii]

Oni jitókome ja dano yote,   *jm* jm *jm* jm   70
 ja zairídioza (daide).   *jm* jii *jm* jii
Jitókome zairide irigi nite (daide),   *jm* jm
 zeda nite (daide),   *jm* jm
 yígie ruite (daide),   *jm* jm
 onókozi ruite (daide),   *jm* jm   75
 irebai ruite (daide).   *jm* jm jm *jm*
Jamáiruiñede,   *jm* jm
 finote.   *jm* jm jm *jm* jm

Réirugo óitioza.   *jm* jm
Oni, ja ua, jíibie dútioza.   *jm* jm   80
Jíibitikoi, kirítikoi nítioza,   *jm* jii
 réirugo óitioza,   *jm*
 imúiforo óitioza,   *jm* jm
 jíibie béeitioza,   *jm* jm
 iáikogo óitioza.   *jm* jm *jm* jm   85

Abina onóiyena,   *jm* jm
 uafue raiyena,   *jm*
 finoyena.   *jm* jm *jm*

                                                      [iii]

Oni rigoza ie   *jm* jm
 kirítikoi, ua jirife kuináyena,   *jm* jii   90
 rigoza ie rabe oyena,   *jm* jm
 rigoza táijie-   *jm*
 -na ite.   *jm* jm
Jebókoro nita dotari,   *jm* jm
 o mirigo júiyie métayena.   *jm* jm *jm* jm jm *jm* jm   95

You won't speak unproperly,
  you will plant cocoyam.
That's what our stomach's for!—
  they are taught   65
  not to touch what belongs to another.
You won't be negligent.
And the girl, truly, knows how to grate manioc,
  she knows how to work.

[ii]

Besides, one teaches the boy the same—   70
  because you are already grown up (one says).
The boy who is growing up weaves an *irigi* fish trap,[3]
  weaves a *zeda* fish trap,[4]
  weaves a trap for tinamous,
  weaves a trap for mice,   75
  weaves a trap for big animals.
He is not negligent,
  he obeys.

You will fetch firewood,
Furthermore, truly, you will *mambe* coca.   80
You will weave a small basket to gather coca leaves,
  you will fetch firewood,
  you will fetch cecropia leaves,
  you will toast coca leaves,
  you will prepare vegetable salt.   85

In order to respect,
  and be truthful,
  and fulfil your duties.

[iii]

On the other hand, the small basket is for the girl,
  for her to tie it with bark strips so that it can be carried;   90
  the girl has to fetch leaves to line it—
  that is the girl's
    work.[5]
Once the boy has woven an open-weave basket, he must throw it away
  so that his sister may use it to store manioc dough.   95

77

Moo úriya   *jm* jm
　komekɨ ífue.   *jm* jm
Ɨnɨaɨ yóñeitɨoza,   *jm* jɨɨ
　ráiraɨfue yóñeitɨoza.   *jm* jm
Fui o yoite buu iñede (daɨde)   *jm* jm   100
　abɨna onóiyena.   *jm* jm *jm jm*
Fui o kue iñeiye mei o úrue ja rɨɡo oyɨnomo (daɨde)   *jm*
　urue komúiteza   *jm* jm
　urue o káadoye táɨneitɨoza.   *jm* jm
Akɨ dɨno yote.   *yote* jm *jm* jm   105

Daaje izoi rɨɡoza,   *jm* jm
　o monoɨ ɨáiyeza,   *jm* jm
　jaɨnoibi óitɨoza,   *jm* jm
　farékajɨ tɨitɨoza,   *jm* jm
　jukui kuáɨtɨoza.   *jm* jm *jm jm jm*   110
Ráiraɨfue yóñeiri   *jm* jm *jm jm*
　kaɨ meáidaiteza,   *jm* jɨɨ
　ebena úriñeitɨoza.   *jm* jm
Yote.   *Yote* jm *jm* jm

                                              [iv]
Ie izoi ite (daɨde).   *jm* jɨɨ *jm* jm   115
Meita jitókome ráɨide (daɨde),   *jm* jm
　moo úriyado kakáreide.   *jm* jm
Daaje izoi jitaɨɡo ráɨide,   *jm* jm
　oni ba jukui kuaɨde.   *jm* jm
Ei abɨ ñekɨro móoi-mooide,   *jm* jɨɨ   120
　amégɨni nite,   *jm* jm
　rafue kakáreide,   *jm* jɨɨ
　ɨnɨñede.   *jm* jm *jm* jm
Ie rɨɡoza   *jm*
　ua kazíyano nóoiri.   *jm* jm *jm jm*   125
Ei úai fɨnote,   *jm*
　moo úai fɨnote,   *jm* jm
　káadoga úrue   *jm* jm
　ɨnɨdoñeɡa úrue.   *jm* jm

The Father's talk,
  the voice of his heart.
You mustn't sleep too much,
  you mustn't be lazy.
Later, there won't be anyone to teach you   100
  how to behave.
Later, when I will no longer be here and you have taken a wife,
  you will have children,
  you will start to look after your children.
One teaches this way.   105

The same for the girl,
  for your breasts to be full of milk
  you will fetch water,
  you will grate sweet manioc,
  you will boil down the juice of bitter manioc.   110
Don't be lazy,
  because you will disgrace us;
  you won't say naughty things.
One teaches.

            [iv]
It is this way (one says).   115
And so, the young man is seated (one says),
  he pays attention to his father's talk.
The girl sits down as well;
  furthermore, she is boiling the juice of bitter manioc.
Next to her mother, she twists and twists *cumare* fibers,   120
  she knits arm bands,
  she pays attention to the teachings,
  she doesn't sleep.
And the girl
  on waking up, bathes.   125
She obeys her mother,
  she obeys her father—
  she is a child who is cared for,
  she is a child who is watched over.

Fɨgo kakáreiri.   *jm* jm *jm* jm   130
Ieka úrue kakade,   *jm* jm
   yetaka úrue,   *jm* jm
   yetaka rɨgoza.   *jm* jm *jm* jm
Fui daaje izoi úruerenia   *jm* jm
   urue yoyɨfuena   *jm*   135
   fɨébite.   *jm* jm
Dɨnomo kakade.   *jm* jm *jm* *jm*

                                                                [v]

Ie izoi eróikano ja
   ua yokana uite.   *jm* jm *jm* jm
Jɨaɨma raa jetai daɨnano,   *jm* jm *jm*   140
   jɨaɨma ie ua
   mei báɨferede.   *jm* jɨɨ *jm*
Ebena úriñede   *jm* jm *jm* jm
   jɨaɨma abɨ fáɨganoiza.   *jm* jɨɨ
Buu úrue,   *jm*   145
   éinide,   *jm*
   móonide,   *jm*
   kuena
      omoɨ dáɨitaiza.   *jm* jm *jɨɨ* *jm*
Yoga.   *jm* jm *jm* jm   150

Akie izoide (daɨde)   *jm* jɨɨ
   idɨ úai   *jm*
   káɨmona
   féeide.   *jm* jm *jm* *jm*
Jae akɨ daɨi éinamakɨ yote,   *jm*   155
   daɨde.   *jm*
Ja úriya   *jm* jɨɨ
   féekuizo   *jm*
   yoga.   *jm* jɨɨ

Nɨɨ kaɨ úrue yófuia úai,   *jm* jm   160
   iedo abɨna onode.   *jm* jɨɨ
Jɨaɨma ie jetáñeno iri,   *jm* jm
   jɨaɨma óogodo jetáñeno iri,   *jm*

Pay close attention! 130
To those teachings the child listens,
  a disciplined boy,
  a disciplined girl.
Later, in the same way, when they have children,
  these teachings will be passed on 135
  to those children.
They listen to this.

                                               [v]

In the same way,
  one continues teaching.
Don't touch that which belongs to another, 140
  because another person's belongings
  will bring problems.
Don't speak unproperly,
  because this will anger others.
Whose child is this? 145
  He has no mother,
  he has no father—
  so they will speak of me
    because of your faults.
It is taught. 150

In this way (one says),
  the true word
  we have
  neglected.
Formerly, thus the ancients taught us, 155
  one says.
Now, that teaching
  is gently
  imparted.

That is the same word to teach our children; 160
  with that they behave.
Don't touch what belong to another,
  don't touch another's plantain,

jɨaɨma jífikoyɨ jetáñeno iri,   *jm*
jɨaɨma jɨrɨ́kue oñeiri,   *jm* jɨɨ *jm jm*   165
jɨkánota oga,   *jm* jɨɨ
ie fɨgora.   *jm* jm *jm* jm *jm* jm
Yetaka úrue kaɨmáfuedo úrite,   *jm* jɨɨ
ebena úriñede.   *jm* jm *jm* jm

                                                                        [III]
Meita jitókome jaka ráɨide,   *jm* jm *jm* jm   170
  jíibie dute,   *jm*
  jíibie béeɨana onode,   *jm*
  jíibie izíyana onode,   *jm*
  jíibie guájana onode,   *jm* jm
  úriyana onode.   *jm* jm *jm* jm *jm* jm   175
Moo izoi komuide,   *jm* jm
  jenode,   *jm* jɨɨ
  jenoka baiga.   *jm* jɨɨ *jm* jm
Ie izóikana jae ñuera úai,   *jm* jm
  jíibina úai dɨona úai.   *jm* jm   180
Ie dɨga   *jm*
  jenode.   *jm* jm *jm* jm
Afekɨ komékɨdo   *jm* jm
  ɨnɨde.   *jm*

Rɨgoza daaje izoi.   *jm* jm *jm*   185
Mazákarɨ mamékɨdo   *jm*
  ɨnɨde.   *jm*
Farékatofe mamékɨdo   *jm*
  ɨnɨde,   *jm* jɨɨ *jm*
  ñúe.   *jm* jm *jm* jm   190

Idɨ úai
  mei jae féeide.   *jm*
Ie jira komo kaɨ jénua,   *jm*
  ñúe.   *jm* jɨɨ
Urúiaɨ komuiya eróikana   *jm* jm *jm* jm   195
  táɨnomo kaɨ óñega,   *jm* jm *jm* jm
  akɨe izoide.   *jm* jɨɨ *jm* jm

don't touch another's sapote,
don't harvest another's forest grapes—   165
ask first, then you can touch it,
  thus it is right.
A disciplined child speaks properly
  he doesn't say naughty things.

                                                                [III]
And so, the young man is seated,   170
  he *mambes* coca,
  he knows how to toast the coca,
  he knows how to strain the coca,
  he knows how to pound the coca,
  he knows how to speak.   175
He grows up like his father,
  he searches,
  and what he searches he finds.
Such was the good word in former times,
  the word of coca and the word of tobacco.   180
With that
  he seeks.
With that heart
  he goes to sleep.

The same for the young woman.   185
With the thought of peanuts
  she goes to sleep.
With the thought of sweet manioc
  she goes to sleep,
  and sleeps well.   190

That true word
  has been neglected.
For this reason, we are just about beginning to seek it,
  for the sake of what is good.
Looking at the children that grow up—   195
  we do not employ it in vain.
  So it is.

Ie mei,
  neemei?   *jm* jm
  jae akɨ daɨi eróikana ñúe arɨ úriyafue bite,   *jm* jm   200
  rɨgoza dɨbene, fɨza dɨbene.   *jm* jɨɨ *jm* jm
Nɨɨ ñuéfuena itɨno dɨona jíibina úai,   *jm*
  farékatofe mazákarɨ úai.   *jm* jɨɨ *jm* jm *jm*
Akie izóikano   *jm* jm *jm*
  arɨ ñúefuena fuite.   *jm* jm *jm* jm *jm* jm jm   205

Bibe 3A

Bainaago rɨgo
jɨfueriraɨgo

[I]

Nɨɨ mei ua
  ja ua
  komuide rɨgo   *jm*
  jɨfueriraɨgo ie mamekɨ.   *jɨɨ* jm
Meita afe rɨgo   5
  ua
  dɨga éinamakɨ jɨfuékano uite,   *jɨɨ* jm
  dɨga jitókome jɨfuékano uite,   *jɨɨ* jm
  afe rɨgo.   *jm* jm
Ie jira buuna   10
  mei oñega,   *jɨɨ* jm
  buuna oñega mei taɨno yófɨrede.   *jɨɨ* jm
Ua ráfuena mei
  jae ua iñega   *Iñega* jm
  afe rɨgo.   *jm* jm   15

Fia meita ua ie mamekɨ ua áiyuena,   *jm* jm
  bainaago.   *Bainaago* jm
Bainaago ie mamekɨ mei ua akɨ ua

Then,
  where did we get it from?
  This same good talk comes from former times,   200
  both for the young woman and the young man.
The same good Word is the word of tobacco and coca,
  the word of sweet manioc and peanut.
In this manner
  the good Word concludes.   205

Text 3A

The Giant Armadillo
is a Deceitful Woman

                  [I]

Then truly, in the same way,
  truly now,
  a woman appeared
  whose name is the Deceiver.
And so that woman,   5
  truly,
  has been deceiving many elders,
  has been deceiving many young men—
  that woman.
For that reason   10
  nobody marries her;
  nobody marries her because she tells many lies.
She didn't receive
  proper instruction,
  that woman.   15

Well, only her name is impressive—
  Bainaaĝo, the Giant Armadillo.
That name *Bainaaĝo* means

bínɨe naaġo, bie énɨe naaġo.   *jm* jm
Ie jira ie mamekɨ bainaaġo.   *jm* jm   20
                                                          [II][i]

Ie jira uafue daɨnano
  jae imakɨ oga.   *jm* jm
Kuemo ua
  mazaka ite, kuemo farékatofe ite, kuemo
  juzítofe ite (daɨde).   25
Kuemo jakaie ite,   *jm* jɨɨ
  kuemo dunajɨ ite, kuemo jifirai ite,   *jm*
  daɨna jira imakɨ oga,   *jm* jm
  uafue daɨnano.   *jm*

Ie jira ja ua   30
  ɨníreide ja ua.   *jm*
Ja ua kɨrɨgaɨ ua áiyue kɨrɨgaɨ niyánona
  ja ie aɨ ite.   *jm* jm
Daɨɨ ñetá ja ua
  ja áɨredɨkue daɨnánona,   35
  ja náɨraɨna amena tɨétate.   *jm*

Uafue daɨnano naɨraɨ ja ua amena tɨede.   *jɨɨ* jm
Tɨédɨmakɨ, ua tɨédɨmakɨ,
  ja ua
  zafénaiya yezika ja jobaiya daɨde.   *jɨɨ* jm   40
Ie jira, mai, daɨde,   *jm* jm
  ja ua jakafaɨ boode, daɨde.   *jɨɨ* jm

Ja mei kɨrɨgaɨ niyánona iga,   *jm* jm
  o táɨjɨɨri rɨġo, daɨde.   *jm* jm
Ie abɨna ua   45
  kɨrɨgaɨ abɨnota ua
  jáaifɨrede,   *jm*
  afeɨe ua jakáfaɨmo.
Ie abɨna dúkɨɨyanona ifo raɨta, raɨta, raɨta, dɨnomo ɨnɨde.   *jm* jm

Mei taɨjɨ́deita ua   50
  fia ɨnɨ́ana onode.   *jm* jm jm

86

"The Mistress of this World."
So, her name is *Bainaago*.   20

[**II**][i]

So, thinking she was a proper woman
  formerly they took her as a wife.
"I have peanuts,
  I have sweet manioc,
  I have bitter manioc," she would say.   25
"I have yam,
  I have cocoyam, I have chili pepper";
  because she spoke this way they took her as a wife,
  thinking it was true.

Then, truly,   30
  she had a husband, now truly.
Now he wove a basket, a big basket,
  and gave it to his wife.
That done, truly now,
  as though saying "I have a wife,"   35
  he had the people clear the jungle.

Thinking it was true, the people cleared the jungle.
They were chopping and chopping
  and then, truly,
  when it got dry they burned it.   40
Then, "It's ready," he said,
  "the field is burnt," he said.

Now that he had woven and given her a basket,
  "Now, woman, you have to work," he said.
But then, truly,   45
  carrying that basket
  she would go
  to that jungle clearing.
However, upon arriving, she would dig a hole and in it she slept.

How was she going to work   50
  if she only knew how to sleep?

Mei kirigai
  ua dunaji uiyena, ua rozídoro uiyena,
  ua jakaiji uiyena, tuburi uiyena,   *jm*
  refiji uiyena,   *jm* jm   55
  ie abina taigai uite.   *jm* jm

                                      [ii]

Iena nibai kue ai taijide dainano eróizaide.
Eróizaide abina ifomo
  iko-ikókiride.   *jm* jm
Nii iko ua bie izoide, daide,   *jm* jm   60
  ja ua, nieze mei ñeite.   *jm*
Ie abido ja bite.   *jii* jm

Dama afémie jíibie ote, dama ua imúiforo ote, atide.   *jii* jm
Atiano jíibie finode.   *jm* jm
Naiona ja úrite.   *jm* jm   65
Figo ua táijiri ua
  juzítofe komúiyena ua,
    mazákari komúiyena, rozídoro komúiyena, jifirai komúiyena,
  jífikona komúiyena,
  jimena komúiyena,   70
  ie ai yófuete.   *jii*

Ie abina daii ja jakáfaimo jáai-jaide,
  fia bite.   *jm* jm
Ja ie ikoimo
  ja jakafai ja niride   75
  ja kiráirena jáaide.   *jm* jm
Fia ua nirítaga,   *jm* jm
  nino minikana iñede.   *jm* jm
Ua afe rairúikana ie jiga júzie ua
  ua fia jaka ua jinóñede.   *jm* jm   80

                                   [iii]

Ie jira ua,
  nieze ítio, daide.   *jii* jm
iráredikue, daide,   *jm*
  énie guiitikue irárena.   *jm* jm

Well, the basket
  is to carry cocoyam, to carry pineapple,
  to carry yam, to carry *daledale,*
  to carry sweet potato;   55
  however she brought it back empty.

                            [ii]

"Perhaps my wife is working," he said and went to look.
He went to look, but in that hole
  she was loudly snoring.
"So, it is like this!" he said.   60
  "Now, what can be done?" he said.
He came back.

He gathered coca leaves and cecropia leaves, and brought them home.
He brought them and prepared *mambe* of coca.
At night he spoke.   65
"You have to work well, truly,
  for bitter manioc to grow, truly,
  for peanut to grow, for pineapple to grow, for chili pepper to grow,
  for sapote to grow,
  for peach palm to grow,"   70
  he admonished his wife.

However, she kept going to the garden
  and returned empty-handed.
Then finally,
  the garden was full of weeds,   75
  it was full of cecropia trees.[1]
She only let weeds grow,
  there was nothing to harvest.
The manioc she planted negligently
  didn't grow well.   80

                          [iii]

And then, truly,
  "What's the matter with you," he said.
"I'm ill," she said,
  "because I eat soil I am ill."

89

Ua daii,   85
  ieikoimo ja afe kirigai dino
  ja ua júzie kigi ie
  bitánokaiga.   *jm*

Daii ñetá jofomo bite.   *jm* jm
Jofomo bite ua,   90
  ua fia.   *jm* jm
Ie jáaide dano
  jakáfaimo jáaiya abina ja ie kirigai iñede.   *jm* jm
Ja ua,
  ja ua baie ua bináaġona ja jáaide.   *jm* jm   95

Dinómona ja ua
  ja mei ua
  táinona úrite ja ua
  uafue riġona ja mei úriñede, fia ua ebe riġona úrite.   *jm* jm
Ie jira ja jino ie ini dotaka,   *jm* jm   100
  fffu, jadí ráiruiginana o jáairi, daide.   *jm* jm
Ja dinomo ja jino batínomo ja
  jukágina naidaide.
Nii mameki ráiraiguna.   *jm* jm

                                                           [iv]
Fui jofórue namaki komúiadedi   105
  dáitade riġo ja jino dotaka dinomo
  ja ua
  ráiraigunana jáaide, daide.   *jm*
Ja ie kirigai ja bináaġona jáaide,   *jm* jm
  ie jana.   *Jana* jm jm   110

Ie jira afénomona ja ua
  ja rafue yoyena.   *jm* jm
Ebena jitókome riġo omoi óiza, daide   *jm* jm
  ímiena omoi jáaiza, daide.   *jm* jm
Riġo eróikano oga, daide,   *jm* jm   115
  jiérede riġo onóirede, daide.   *jii* jm

And so,   85
  finally she abandoned that basket
  there,
  in the middle of the garden,

That done, she came home.
She came home, truly,   90
  with nothing.
She went back again
  to the garden, but the basket was no longer there.
Now truly,
  that basket had turned into a giant armadillo.   95

From then on,
  truly,
  she tells lies,
She doesn't speak like a proper woman, she speaks like a wicked
                                           woman
For that reason her husband threw her into the forest,   100
  "Pff! turn into a black termites' nest," he said.
Now, there out in the forest
  she exists as a termites' nest.
That same is called "the lazy woman."

                                                   [iv]
Later on, when the new generations grow up—   105
  "That kind of woman was thrown into the forest
  and there, truly,
  she turned into a termites' nest," they will say.
"Now, her basket turned into a giant armadillo,
  it is its portrait."   110

Well, from all that
  there is a lesson to be learnt.
"Boys, if you foolishly choose a woman,
  what happened to him will also happen to you," one says.
"Be watchful when choosing a woman," one says,   115
  "a hard-working woman can be recognized," one says.

Jifirai rite, taikadu taite ua,
  mazákari taikadu ite,
  ua farékatofe jite, ua rozídoro rite,
  nii mei úa riƓo, daide.   *jm* jm   120
Fui eróiñeno riƓo omoi óiadi daii omoi zefuiri, daide.   *jm* jm

Nii ja ua
  diga jitókome jifuékano uite.   *jm* jm
Akie izóikana ja ite
  afeƓo mameki.   *jm*   125

[III]

Ie mei baie ua
  duera ñeniƓo ba ua
  uániƓo.   *jm* jm
Baie
  jiaie ba   130
  nákoniƓo.   *jm* jm

Baie ua
  jiérede riƓo kirigai,   *jii* jm
  ibigai mei
  mazákari ie jóoneyena.   *jm* jm   135
Jiaie kirigai mameki
  kovero,   *Kovero* jm kovero
  baie
  jifiji ie jóoneyena.   *jm* jm

Dinori baie ua   140
  kirigai ibigai komuide,   *jm* jm
  jiérede riƓo ie.   *jm* jm
Dinómona ja ua jitókome
  afe kirigai nite,   *jm* jm
  ibigai,   *Ibigai* jm   145
  ñenigai.   *Ñenigai* jm

Ie mei baie jebogai,   *jm*

92

"She sows chili pepper, she digs up the ground,
  for peanuts she digs a plot,
  she plants sweet manioc, she plants pineapple;
  that's a proper woman," one says.   120
"If you then choose a woman carelessly, the same will happen to you,"
                  one says.

That same woman, truly,
  has been deceiving many young men.
Therefore this is
  that woman's name.   125

[III]

But that
  small *ñenïgo* armadillo, that is
  the proper armadillo.
That other one
  is also proper, that   130
  spurred armadillo.

That is truly
  the hard-working woman's basket,
  the *ibigaï* basket,[2]
  the one to store peanuts.   135
Another basket is called
  kovero,[3]
  that one
  is to store chili peppers.

From there   140
  the *ibigaï* basket appeared,
  the hard-working woman's one.
From then on, the young man now
  weaves that kind of basket,
  the *ibigaï*   145
  and *ñenigaï.*[4]

But that *jebogaï* basket[5]

baie dáɨita zefuide rɨǥo igaɨ,   *jm* jɨɨ
bainaaǥo
  ie kɨrɨgaɨ,   *jm*   150
jebogaɨ,   *jebogaɨ* jm
jujɨ ua jóoneyena,   *jm*
magajɨ metáyena,   *jm* jm
meita oñega,
raɨre ráataite.   *jm* jm   155
Daa akie mamekɨ fɨébiya,   *jm*
  jebogaɨ.   *jm* jm

                                                                    [**IV**]

Akie izoi
  mei rɨǥo
  jɨfuefɨrede rɨǥo mameka.   *jm*   160
Táɨjɨe iñede, mɨnɨka mei yoite.   *jm* jɨɨ
Fia ua abɨ uikaide,   *jm* jm
  táɨnofue yokaide.   *jm* jɨɨ

Ie jiyákɨmo ja batɨnomo ja
  ja nogoraɨ jɨrénote   165
  afeǥo.   *jm* jɨɨ
Ja jino mei dotaka ja jiyákɨmo jáaide.   *jm* jɨɨ
Dɨnomo ja
  tiii-ri-ri-ri-ri-ri,
  ba ie mona gɨrɨ̃ia   *jm* jɨɨ   170
  bainaaǥo gɨrɨ̃taga.   *jm* jm
Nana ua
  bie énɨe ua
  tiii-ri-ri-ri-ri-ri, daɨna yezika bie énɨe ua
  dokaide.   *jɨɨ* jm   175
Dɨnomo ja afeǥo
  ja ana raɨnade.   *jm* jm
Akie izoide.   *jm* jm

that's the basket of this story's woman,
the giant armadillo's
  basket. 150
The *jebogaɨ* basket
is to store bitter manioc tubers
and to hold manioc dough,[6]
but one does not keep the basket
because it wears out quickly. 155
Only its name remains:
  jebogaɨ basket.

                        [IV]

In that manner
  a woman,
    a deceitful woman, gets her name. 160
She doesn't work, what can she speak of?
In vain she has a good body,
  she only tells lies.

Out there, in the Bottom of this World,[7]
  she spins a big earthenware pot— 165
  that woman.
When she was cast out she went to the Bottom of this World.
There,
  when a thunder sounds:
  "tiii-ri-ri-ri-ri-ri," 170
  it is the giant armadillo's thunder.[8]
Truly, all of
  this land, truly,
  when it sounds "tiii-ri-ri-ri-ri-ri," all of this land
  trembles. 175
There, she
  settled down.
So it is.

"WORD ON DISCIPLINE"
"THE GIANT ARMADILLO IS A DECEITFUL WOMAN"

The word *yetárafue,* Uitoto title of text 3, contains the same root *ye-* ("behavior") that forms the word *yera,* "tobacco paste."[1] The tobacco paste is a symbol of a man's word and his discipline. This paste dissolved in water, for instance, is given, as a drink, to unruly persons as a punishment and a remedy. Breaking down the word *yetárafue* into its morphemes, we obtain: *ye-,* "behavior"; *-ta-,* "to cause to"; and *-ra-fue,* "Word/Thing" (see discussion of the term *rafue* in the commentary on text 1). *Yetárafue* can thus be interpreted as "Word on causing to behave, or on discipline." Some Indians translate it as "Word of counsel," but I prefer the stronger connotation of "discipline," which is confirmed by Preuss who glosses the root *yeta* as "to frighten, to scare away, to scold, to startle."[2]

After chapter 2, that dealt with "the part of the Mother," there comes this text on "the words of the Father's Leaf" (line 1) to startle the young people into behaving well. The "Leaf" refers to the tobacco leaf, the root of discipline; it is also the Father's tongue that utters the Word on discipline.

Yetárafue is the set of norms necessary to be a true man; likewise, it is the base of *rafue.* "Without *yetárafue* a young man cannot use that Word [of dance rituals or of healing], without *yetárafue* that Word damages the person," Kɨneraɨ says.

Every activity has its own rules of *yetárafue.* There is *yetárafue* for a man to *mambe* coca, for the pregnant woman, for the father of a newly born child, and so forth. Every food one eats and every activity one carries out has a potential effect on life. For this reason, all the activities and behavior of young people are carefully controlled. These rules have the effect of instilling the need for proper behavior in young people by scaring them with the potential negative effects that, it is assured, certain acts of conduct will bring forth.

This form of social control has slowly eroded during the last 80 years as a result of the violence associated with rubber exploitation, forced resettlements, christianization, and a growing dependence on the market economy. This is deeply felt by the older Indians, who see how the younger generations do not follow the basic rules of *yetárafue.* Likewise Kɨneraɨ says (lines 151-159):

In this way (one says),
the true word
we have
neglected.
Formerly, thus the ancients taught us,

96

one says.
Now, that teaching
  is gently
  imparted.

And for this reason, this instruction is sought again (lines-191-197):

That true word
  has been neglected.
For this reason, we are just about beginning to seek it,
  for the sake of what is good.
Looking at the children that grow up—
  we do not employ it in vain.
  So it is.

Yetárafue is one of the most complex subjects of Indian thought. In this text Kɨneraɨ just enunciates the major headings of tobacco *yetárafue*, namely: kinship, young people's work and behavior, and the word of tobacco and coca. These subjects correspond to the three parts that can be recognized in the text, which I have marked with upper-case Roman numerals on the right margin of the page. I have furthermore divided part II in five sections, identified with lower-case Roman numerals.

Siblings, Grandparents, and Uterine Uncle

Part I provides a brief outline of consanguineous relatives, which is in fact a statement of rules of marriage. Marriage is exogamic, that is what he means in the second stanza (lines 9-13):

Boy, this is your sister,
  girl, this is your brother,
  one says.
So that they start
  learning how to behave.

Uitoto terms of kinship for siblings vary according to personal gender. Thus, there are two terms to say "my sister"; one if the speaker is a man, another if the speaker is a woman. In this case, when he says "your sister" he is referring to a man's sister, and when he says "your brother" he is referring to a woman's brother. The first rule of behavior is to be able to recognize the non-marriageable relatives: for a man, his sister; for a woman, her brother.

He then proceeds to explain who a man's "sisters" and a woman's "brothers" are. He first establishes the difference between paternal and maternal relatives, and places the emphasis on paternal "cousins." Sisters and brothers include all paternal cousins: these are non-marriageable relatives (see lines 14-29).

In the relations with paternal relatives the main concern is the discrimination of non-marriageable relatives. In the relations with parents and grandparents and with maternal relatives the concern is with recognition and respect. The marked differentiation between relatives on the paternal and maternal sides derives from the virilocal form of residence and the patrilineal mode of filiation among the Uitoto and other neighboring tribes.[3] A virilocal form of residence means that the woman goes to live next to her husband's family; and a patrilineal mode of filiation means that the children belong to their father's group or "clan" (*ízie* or *inairai*), not their mother's. For this reason a child grows up next to his/her paternal relatives and belongs to their same clan, whereas his/her maternal relatives live away from him/her and belong to a different clan—the mother's clan, which is not the child's.

Thus, a marked attitude of respect toward the maternal uncle is a social means of expressing and reinforcing the relation of alliance with the clan to which the child's mother belongs. Similarly, respect and recognition towards grandparents express and reinforce the bonds of filiation (of belonging to the group). This double recognition of the bonds of alliance and filiation is what the fourth and fifth stanzas express (see lines 30-43).

Here, Kinerai makes reference to the grandmother, the grandfather, and the maternal uncle. In all three cases it is said that the child should not address any of them by their names—i.e. their personal names. This is a rule of politeness, valid also for all relatives and non-relatives: one should never address anybody by his/her personal name but by a term of kinship or some form of indirect address.[4] Even more so, it would be highly unpolite to address grandparents or a maternal uncle with a term different from that of kinship.

Young people should also be gentle (see line 33) when addressing their elders. The reason is given in lines 37-38: "So as not to upset the elders, / one keeps teaching them." The expression "to upset" only partially conveys the meaning of the Uitoto verb *abi fáigakaide* which literally means "to get startled." Kinerai explains: "The body and the heart of older men, who use a lot of tobacco and coca, are hot; you have to address them gently and properly, because if you 'startle their heart' that heat of theirs will be projected onto your body and will take the form of an illness." This explains the last verse of the fifth stanza (lines 42-43): "They are taught / to take care of themselves."

Boys' and Girls' Behavior and Work

The subject of part II is clearly indicated by its opening stanza (lines 44-49):

"The boy who grows up
opens up a food-plot in an abandoned jungle clearing"

From then on,
   it is like this (one says).
The boy who grows up
   must behave himself.
The girl who grows up, one says,
   must behave herself.

When boy and girl reach the age of reason and have learnt to recognize their relatives, the instruction on proper work and behavior begins.

   The thirteen stanzas that compose this part alternate between advice for males and females, with stanzas functioning as refrains placed between them. Through this alternation of stanzas, five main themes—marked as sections with lower-case Roman numerals—are developed, each one with its particular rhythm.

"Furthermore, you will weave a small basket"
(Photograph by Marta L. Torres)

Section i, after the opening refrain, presents the most meaningful labors of both sexes in agricultural work. The young man has to know how to clear the jungle in order to till a food-plot, and to weave the basketry utensils necessary to harvest and process the plot's products. The young woman has to know how to plant and tend the plot.

Usually, a tract of mature forest is cleared for a new food-plot. This is a difficult task which often requires the participation of men from other families. In order to gauge his strength against the forest, a boy should start alone and only attempt to clear a small plot of fallow land, that is, an old, abandoned food-plot. In this plot he will plant tobacco and coca, whose seeds he receives from his father, and sweet manioc, whose seeds he receives from his mother. From then on, he will prepare his own tobacco paste, will elaborate his own *mambe* of coca, and will have the seeds of sweet manioc for his future wife.

But to get a wife he needs to know how to weave. Basketry and weaving stand as a metaphor of exogamy and marriage.[5] The "wedding ring" that a young man has to offer to a young woman for marriage is precisely what Kɨnerai tells about in lines 52-55:

Furthermore, you will weave a small basket (one says),
  you will weave a basket (one says),
  you will weave a manioc sieve (one says),
  you will weave a manioc strainer (one says).

100

Open-weave basket *jebogai*
(bottom view)

Open-weave basket *jebogai*
(side view)

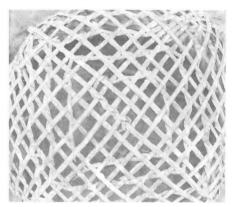

Narrow-weave basket *ibigai*
(bottom view)

Narrow-weave basket *ibigai*
(side view)

Narrow-weave basket *ñenigai*
(bottom view)

Narrow-weave basket *ñenigai*
(side view)

There are two main types of carrying baskets among the Uitoto, Okaina and Bora, which stand for two kinds of women: (1) an open-weave basket with a three-strand lattice base and walls intertwined with a thread; this is called *jebogaɨ* and it stands for a lazy and deceitful woman; and (2) a narrow-weave basket made of paired standards[6] intertwined by a twisting thread, which is called *ibigaɨ;* a variation of this type of basket, called *ñenɨgaɨ,* is made by two sets of four standards woven in spiral and also intertwined by a twisting thread—this is made by the Okaina and Bora people, not by the Uitoto; these baskets stand for a hard-working woman.

The first type of basket is said to be the "portrait" of the giant armadillo, the second the portrait of the small armadillo. The type of basket a young man should weave is the second, "the one of the hard-working woman," as Kɨneraɨ says in the story of the giant armadillo, which I include in text 3A.

This distinction between types of baskets, and its corresponding types of women, seems to mark the extent to which exogamous marriage is allowed; beyond that limit, only "deceitful" women will be found. It is possible that the two weaving techniques serve to demarcate a cultural frontier between the tribes living south of the Caquetá river (Uitoto, Okaina, Bora, Muinane, Miraña, and Andoke) and those living north (tribes of the Arawak and Eastern Tukano linguistic groups). The *ibigaɨ* basket—the hard-working woman's one—is made by Uitoto, Bora, and Okaina; it does not appear north of the Caquetá. On the other hand, a basket woven with a similar technique to the Uitoto's *jegobaɨ*—the deceitful woman's basket—is elaborated by Arawak and Tukano tribes.

Now, in the woman's role, the emphasis is on her agricultural skills. After the men have cleared and burnt a tract of jungle, it is the women's responsibility to plant the new food-plot, keep it clean, and harvest its products. This is clearly expressed in the story of the giant armadillo (text 3A, lines 38-44):

They were chopping and chopping
  and then, truly,
  when it got dry they burned it.
Well then, "It's ready," he said,
  "the field is burnt," he said.
Now that he had woven and given her a basket,
  "Now, woman, you have to work," he said.

The woman of that story—an "unproper" woman—failed in planting and taking care of the garden, and abandoned the basket that her husband had woven and given to her. Because of that, her husband repudiated her and turned her into a termites' nest. This is the kind of woman a young man should not take as a wife.

The key of the distinction between a "proper" and an "unproper" woman has to do with agricultural skills. All Indian groups of the Putumayo, Caquetá, and

The Deceitful Woman

Later on, when the new generations grow up—
"That kind of woman was thrown into the forest
and there, truly,
she turned into a termites' nest," they will say.
"Now, her basket turned into a giant armadillo,
it is its portrait."

103

"A hard-working woman can be recognized"

Vaupés basins—with the exception of the Maku Indians—are agricultural peoples and all of them grow more or less the same set of basic cultivated crops. There are, nevertheless, certain crops that are only grown by, or are the specialization of, certain groups. These plants serve to mark the differences among ethnic groups. A proper woman is not only the one who has agricultural skills but also the one who has the specific skills for growing those plants that mark a distinction with other groups.[7] In this case, Kɨnerai emphasizes the skills related to the cultivation of sweet manioc, chili pepper, and, especially, peanuts. He says in text 3 (lines 58-61)—"On the girl's part":

> you will dig up a piece of land
> > to sow chili,
> > to sow peanut,
> > to plant sweet manioc.

And more emphatically in text 3A (lines 115-120):

> "Be watchful when choosing a woman," one says,
> > "a hard-working woman can be recognized," one says.
> "She sows chili pepper, she digs up the ground,
> > "for peanuts she digs a plot,
> > "she plants sweet manioc, she plants pineapple;
> > "that's a proper woman," one says.

Bitter manioc and other tubers are planted in the garden without digging the ground or clearing the fallen trees. The cultivation of peanuts, in contrast, demands a well-tilled plot, free of trunks and stones, and arranged in rows with drainage ditches. In addition, one has to add ashes to this soil. Peanut cultivation demands a lot of work and is thus highly valued. It is to this kind of work that he refers when he says: "she digs up the ground." Arawak and Tukano-speaking groups do not grow peanuts; it only occurs among the groups living south of the Caquetá river.

Yetárafue in relation to male and female work in agriculture contains an implicit statement of ethnic identity, demarcating the limits of "propriety" for behavior and marriage alliances. This is marked, for men, in basketry; for women, in the skills related to growing certain cultivated crops.

Section ii has three stanzas. One refers to hunting traps, the second to the preparation of coca and vegetable salt, and the third is a refrain.

Hunting has a meaning that goes beyond the acquisition of food. "Tobacco hunting" consists of making dawn in the body of animals that which first manifests itself as illness, rage, negligence, quarreling, and so forth. Food is only a by-product of this sort of hunting. As such, the preparation of tobacco and coca are as closely related to hunting as are the setting up of traps. Tobacco and coca are actual hunting weapons.

This can be better illustrated with a text in which Kinerai explains how he trapped some animals that were the cause of problems for him and for his family when he settled in the place where he lives today. He hunted these animals (problems) with tobacco, coca, and traps. I include this text, "On How the Elders Clean the Place Where They Will Live" (3B), with a separate commentary.

Section iii also contains three stanzas. The first refers to a girl's preparation for maternity in a very metaphorical way. Her "small basket" may refer to her womb, to which she must tie bark strips and which she must line with leaves so as to make it an useful sheath to hold food (children). Men weave baskets for women to work with; but men only weave the structure. Women have to finish them—"that is the girl's / work" (lines 92-93).

In the second verse of the first stanza he warns the young man (lines 94-95):

"The small basket is for the girl, for her to tie it with bark strips"

105

> Once the boy has woven an open-weave basket, he must throw it away
> so that his sister may use it to keep manioc dough.

He refers here to the *jebogai* basket, which symbolizes a woman the young man should not marry—an "unproper" woman. That kind of woman would only be useful "for his sister to store manioc dough." That is, if a man chooses such a kind of woman, it should be only as a servant of his female relatives, not as a proper wife.

After this "adolescent" phase—in which the woman makes herself ready for procreation and the man casts aside unproper women—the other two stanzas deal with the guidelines for the new life. Men have to watch over (second stanza) as women have to provide milk (third stanza). Both roles convey complex *yetárafue* rules which here are only sketched. A typical formulation is given to women (lines 106-110):

> The same for the girl,
> for your breasts to be full of milk
> you will fetch water,
> you will grate sweet manioc,
> you will boil down the juice of bitter manioc.

All are activities that demand the manipulation of abundant liquids.

Section iv is one long stanza that contains a succession of advice for both sexes, and illustrates the way they will have to talk to their own children. Musically, this stanza develops as a string of short verses intoned in a similar way. This recitative alludes, with a great economy, to the everyday repetition of advice. In contrast to other "Words," *yetárafue* is not recited once or on special occasions. This is a Word that enters by repetition in the course of everyday life.

The verbs Kinerai uses to say "is seated" and "pays attention" are the same I discuss in the commentary on text 3B, which refers to the cleaning of the place "where children will sleep." This section iv thus alludes to the mode of behavior proper to adulthood, which enables a man and a woman to take care of a family and establish themselves independently in a new setting.

Section v, finally, refers to relationships with other people. The first stanza deals with male behavior, although it is not explicit. Kinerai explains that when he says "Don't touch that which belongs to another" (line 140), he is actually meaning another person's *wife*. The seriousness of the matter is stressed next (lines 145-149):

> Whose child is this?
> He has no mother,
> he has no father—

106

Squeezing the juice of bitter manioc

so they will speak of me
because of your faults.

The second stanza validates these teachings by alluding to their antiquity: "Formerly, thus the ancients taught us" (line 155).

The third, again refers to other people's belongings. In this case, it is addressed to women in relation to not stealing food from another's plot.

The Word of Tobacco, Coca, Sweet Manioc, and Peanut

Part II, which we just reviewed, contains the norms of behavior that will allow young men and women to become responsible adults able to work, bring up a family, and respect other people. The opening stanzas of part III portray those models of man and woman. The young man "is seated," (lines 170-184)

he *mambes* coca,
he knows how to toast the coca,
he knows how to strain the coca,
he knows how to pound the coca,

107

he knows how to speak.
He grows up like his father,
  he searches,
  and what he searches he finds.
Such was the good word in former times,
  the word of coca and the word of tobacco.
With that
  he seeks.
With that heart
  he goes to sleep.
And the young woman (lines 186-190):
  With the thought of peanut
   she goes to sleep.

Bibe 3B

Jae éinamakɨ imakɨ
iyɨno fɨnua úai yoina

[i]

Mei fueñe beno,
  ua beno ua kue
  túuizaɨbiya yezika, *jm* jm
Nɨɨ mei ua
  ua ba beno ua jae ua ite   5
  ua náɨraɨna mameide. *jm* jm
Ie jira beno
  ua fɨnua izoi
  ua ɨáɨena itɨno. *jm* jm
Ie ɨáɨena ite íadɨ mei   10
  naɨ onóinide. *jm* jm

Iémona ja ua
  jae mei éinamakɨ ua ba yúa *jm*
  ua úrue ua ɨnɨyɨno ua rafónori, *jm*

108

With the thought of sweet manioc
  she goes to sleep,
  and sleeps well.

This Word on Discipline has its roots in the four main cultivated crops. For the man, tobacco and coca; for the woman, sweet manioc and peanut. Kɨnerai gathers up the Word of the Father's Leaf and returns it back to its origin—the Mother, the agricultural work—to conclude (lines 199-203):

Where did we get it from?
  This same good talk, comes from former times
  both for the young woman and the young man.
The same good Word is the word of tobacco and coca,
  the word of sweet manioc and peanut.

Text 3B

On How the Elders Clean the Place
Where They Will Live

[i]

Then, so it was here
  when I first came
  to found this place.
So, truly,
  it appeared that there had been others here   5
  who were like the inhabitants of this place.
For this reason, here
  one had to clean
  the filth that was here.
There was filth indeed but   10
  still one couldn't perceive it.

That is why, truly,
  the ancient people had the saying:
  "Clean up where your children will sleep,"

jae éinamakɨ daɨde.   *jm* jm   15
Ie abɨna mei jofo ero
    ua ráfua yoñede,   *jm* jɨɨ
    jino bie ɨáɨena iya,   *jm* jm
    ba réɨkɨna ite, ba okóziena ite, ɨráfuena itɨno.   *jm* jm
Ie jira ua   20
    ja beno méiñotɨkue.   *jm*
Ua jae mei éinamakɨ ua járuigano beno,   *jm* jm
    méiñote ua
    ja ua írea ruitɨkue.   *jm* jm
Ruitɨkue ua   25
    ja ua fuitádɨkue.   *jm* jm

                                      [ii]

Ie baɨfe   *jm*
    ja naɨo dɨbénemo
    ja móomana abɨ fakade.   *jm* jm
Mooma daɨde,   *jm*   30
    nɨbái kue io ɨbáidɨo, daɨde,   *jm* jm
    ɨko kuena moo dáɨñedɨo, daɨde,   *jm* jm
    kuena ɨáɨruitɨo, daɨde.   *jm*
Ie yojérugo oróikana ikɨrite,   *jm* jm
    ua jaka nɨ́imɨe.   *jm* jm   35
Daɨi daɨnano dobáikaide meine jáaide, daɨde.   *jm* jm

Ie kue kazíyano yotɨkue,   *jm* jm
    móomana nɨkáɨritɨkue,
    mooma kue ikɨde ie io kue ɨbaiya jira.   *jm* jm
Mei ua, daɨde.   *jm* jm   40
Mei guita fuita ja jáaikaidɨkoko.   *jm*
Jáaidɨkokomo ráɨide   *jm*
    jirako   *jm*
    ɨima,   *jm*
    éɨbado jíide.   *jm*   45

Ie ua jatágɨdo kue putájiya abɨna batɨ́nena
    aaa, kuemo
    ua kuemo ua zokuade,   *jm*

110

the ancients used to say.   15
But this does not mean
   that you must clean inside the house,
   that filth is out there, in the forest;
   out there, there is fire,[1] there is fatigue, there is illness.
Well then, truly,   20
   I examined this place.
The ancients were afraid of this place,
   I truly examined it;
   then I set up traps.
I set up traps   25
   and put an end to it.

               [ii]

Later on,
   during the night
   something came in the form of my father.
My father said,   30
   "Why did you block my path?" he said,
   "You don't recognize me as your father!" he said,
   "You hate me!" he said.
He was furious, holding a little machete in his hand;
   it looked just like him!   35
Having said that, he turned around and left.

On waking up I told my wife,
   "I dreamed of my father,
   my father was furious with me because I'd blocked his path."
"Is that so?" she said.   40
We finished eating and went to check the trap.
We went, and there it was sitting
   an ocelot,
   a male,
   caught by a foot.   45

I was about to hit it with the axe handle, but from there,
   haa! it jumped
   towards me,

ia kuena baitáñede. *jm*
Abɨ fɨnote, daɨnano   50
  ragɨ ua ota ua afedo ie ɨfo
  puta, *jm*
  dɨno ja ua ana báɨide. *jm*
Ua dɨno nana ua takofo ua
  ígɨaɨ ua fia ua bote, *jm* jm   55
  ie ja ótɨkoko. *jm* jm
Ua bie móomana abɨ fakaja,
  daɨdɨkue. *jm*

Ja ua bítɨkoko
  ua aféɨe   60
  donida ua ja ie igoɨ uánona oni koko dotaka iyemo. *jm* jm
Ie kue dano ráɨidɨkue. *jm* jm

                                         [iii]

Ráɨidɨkue
  dano afe onífene
  ua káigɨa abɨna   65
  kue eɨba ero airágɨtaide. *jm* jm
Ieri izídɨkue, *jm*
  nɨno ua bedáɨitana. *jm* jm
Ɨnɨaidɨkuemo
  ja ua inɨbikaidɨkuemo   70
  ja daa eirɨgo bite. *jm* jm
Ie jira,
  moo, daɨde, *jm*
  jae bizíkɨdo jáaikaidɨkue, daɨde, *jm* jm
  beno náɨgodɨkue, daɨde, *jm*   75
  ikue bie izóikano zefuiya, daɨde. *jm* jm
Ie dɨrɨaɨ ikoro oróoide, *jm*
  éekano jáaide. *jm*

Jitɨramo yotɨkue, *jm*
  éirɨgona nɨkáɨritɨkue. *jm* jm   80
Ie jira, ua, daɨde. *jm*
Guita fuita

but it couldn't reach me.
"A tough guy?" I said to myself.   50
  I cut a stick and on its head
  I hit it!
  Right there it fell down.
It fell breaking all the trap's
  sticks and ropes into pieces;   55
  then we took it away from there.
"Truly, this is the one that took my father's form,"
  I said.

Then we came back,
  we skinned it,   60
  and after peeling its skin off we threw the carcass into the river.
And again I sat down.
                                                  [iii]

I sat down
  and when I was
  weeding near the trap   65
  I injured the sole of my foot.
"Why did I hurt myself?
  What does it mean?" I said.
When I went to sleep that night,
  when I was already falling asleep,   70
  then, an old woman came.
Well then,
  "Son," she said,
  "I have been walking in this forest for a long time," she said,
  "I am the mistress of this place," she said,   75
  "and look at what's happening to me," she said.
She was holding some ants in a wrapper of leaves
  and she walked away crying.

Next morning, I told my wife,
  "I dreamed of an old woman."   80
Well then, "Is it so?" she said.
We finished eating

113

dano káizaidɨkoko.   *jm*
Káizaidɨ-
-kokomo dɨno   85
ja eirɨgo
ja monaide.   *jm* jm

Aɨ, daɨde,   *jm*
ereño jíiya, daɨde.   *jm*
Mena jíidena eroide   *jm*   90
ie abɨna ie oda.   *jm* jm
Ie jino zonoda
ua koko átɨa.   *jm*
Bie daɨi úriya,   *jm* jm
ie mei ja oga, daɨde.   *jm* jm   95
                                                      [iv]

Iémona kakáreidɨkue dano.   *jm*
Kakáreidɨkue ua
áiyue kɨrɨgaɨ
afénomo
monaite,   100
daɨde mɨnɨka kuena.   *jm*
Ie abɨna,
ɨko, bainaago yote.   *jm*
Ie eróizaidɨkokomo   *jm*
bainaago jíiya.   *jm* jm   105
Ie atɨ́dɨkoko,   *jm* jm
ie iyemo koko dotaka.   *jm*
                                                      [v]

Ie dano
kakáreidɨkue.   *jm* jm
Kakáreidɨkue dano,   110
ja nɨkaɨna úrite.   *jm* jm
Kɨnaimo ua joodɨkokomo
ja boraɨgo bite.   *jm*
Bite ua
ua jaka zadáikano bite.   *jm* jm   115
Zadáikano bite ua jaka meáiruiñeno koko abɨ zojode.   *jm*

114

and again we went to check the trap.
On going to check it
  there she was—   85
  now the old woman
  had dawned.

"Ah!" I said.
  "A giant anteater was trapped," I said.
It looked as if two of them had been trapped,   90
  but that was because of its large tail.[2]
We pulled it out
  and brought it home.
"This is the one that talked that way,
  but now we have got it," I said.   95
                                          [iv]

After that, again, I was paying attention.
I was paying attention and
  something told me that,
  "A big basket
  will dawn,   100
  in the trap."
But,
  of course, that meant a giant armadillo.
When we went to look
  a giant armadillo had fallen into the trap.   105
We brought it back
  and threw it into the river.
                                        [v]

Again,
  I was paying attention.
I was again paying attention and   110
  something spoke in a dream.
We were both lying in the hammock
  when a Bora Indian woman came by.[3]
She came by,
  all smiling she came.   115
She came smiling and shamelessly she laid down beside us.

Ie jira oni ii,
  kue aɨ dɨga itɨkue,
  daɨdɨkue. *jm*
Ba fɨnoñeno ua   120
  ba ua kuchúakade izoide. *jm*
Ie jira, oni ii, oni ii, daɨde,
  ja arɨ kue ñuitaka. *jm*
Ie naidakaida ja ua jáaide, *jm*
  ua fúe ua jideka ñúe   125
  ua ekuri *jm*
  ua fɨnobite,
  ie jáaide. *jm*
Meine abɨdo gɨré-gɨre eróikaide. *jm*

Ie yotɨkue, ua akɨ daɨi nɨkáɨritɨkue, *jm*   130
  minɨka nɨbaɨ koko irebaimo jíiya. *jm*
Eróizaidɨkoko,
  jáaidɨkoko.
Jáaidɨkokomo ua
  duera rɨgo   135
  jirako, *jm*
  ie fekábedo jíide. *jm*
Bie ua ja naɨo úriya, daɨde, *jm*
  íadɨ mei ja ofide, daɨde. *jm*

Akɨ daɨi eróikano   140
  jae ua
  beno
  dáɨitadɨno
  ua monáitakano
  kue uiga. *jm* jm   145
                      [vi]

Iraɨe ua
  jino bene jáaikaidɨkaɨ *jm*
  ua zɨokaɨ ua kue onoɨ ero dete. *jm*
Ie afai jáaiyena dano
  jɨáɨe ero jobéyena   150

116

Well then, "Get out!
  I'm with my wife,"
  I said.
She didn't mind   120
  and it seemed she wanted to tickle me.
Well then, "Get out! Get out!" I said
  and pushed her out.
She stood up and went away—
  with her mouth well painted   125
  with red,
  well dressed—
  she went away.
She would turn round, again and again, to look at me.

I told my wife, "I had this dream,   130
  what might have fallen into our trap?"
We went to look,
  we went.
When we arrived,
  a small female   135
  ocelot
  had been caught by its shoulder.
"This one spoke last night," I said,
  "but it has already been trapped," I said.

In this manner,   140
  those
  which came here
  to speak in that way
  were the animals
  I made dawn.   145
                                        [vi]

Finally,
  when we were walking back here
  I cut my hand with a thorny bush.
Again, in order to go upriver to La Chorrera
  I went to cut a yaripa palm[4]   150

jɨkɨfena úaidɨkue.   *jm*
Ie kueri kuadade   *jm*
　jubene ua kaifo fɨébite.   *jm*
Ie kue kota abɨna ua kue ui putáikaide,   *jm*
　ua dɨno fia ana raɨnade.   *jm*   155
Ie kue ui dɨaide,   *jm*
　nɨbaɨ fiide, daɨdɨkue.   *jm*

Ie
　naɨo
　ráɨidɨkue.   *jm*   160
Iemo *compadre* Mánaɨdɨkɨ-   *jm*
　-na bite.   *jm* jɨɨ
Compa, daɨde,   *jm* jm
　jae bie jazíkɨdo féeireitɨkue omo dúkɨna, daɨde.   *jm* jm
Ua jaka nɨɨmɨe.   *jm*   165

Compa, be kue yerakɨ, daɨde.   *jm*
Ie yɨɨnota
　eróidɨkuemo dɨga ebígɨroɨ iya.   *jm* jm
Ie jira
　ana kue raɨnaka.   *jm*   170
Iena meáiruiyano yɨɨnota jáaide,   *jm* jm
　ua jaka yoñede   *jm*
　ua jáaide.
Ua jáaide jaka
　irébaimo jiide   *jm*   175
　janáyari.   *jm* jm
Bie Mánaɨdɨkɨna abɨ fakade.   *jm* jm

Ja mei jiide abɨna Nofɨkomo jáaidɨkoko.   *jm* jm
Dɨnomo
　ja ua
　monaide.   *jm* jɨɨ   180
Meita
　afe izoi itɨno

for the canoe's cross-pieces.
The palm split in half,
  but the broken half remained upright.
As I cut it, it hit me in the eye
  and it stayed upright.   155
My eye was bleeding.
  "Perhaps it has burst," I said.

That
  night
  I sat down.   160
Then it came as my *compadre*[5]
  Mánaɨdɨkɨ.[6]
"Compa," he said,
  "I've been lost for a long time in this forest but now I found you," he
                                                          said.
It looked just like him!   165

"Compa, here is my tobacco paste," he said.
I received it, and
  looking into it I saw it was full of glowworms.
Well then,
  I put it down.   170
He was ashamed, he took his tobacco and went away;
  he didn't say a word,
  he just left.
He truly went
  to fall into the trap,   175
  as a jaguar.
That was the one that took Mánaɨdɨkɨ's form.

When it fell into the trap, we'd already left for La Chorrera.
There,
  truly,   180
  it dawned.
For this reason,
  those things

119

akɨ dáɨita,
ua ba onóiñenia naɨraɨ úriya daɨnana eroide.   *jm* jm   185
Ja mei ua
    kue fakaka
    akɨ daɨi ja birui
    akɨ daɨi kue yoga.   *jm* jm

COMMENTARY ON TEXT 3B:

"ON HOW THE ELDERS CLEAN THE PLACE WHERE THEY WILL LIVE"

In this text Kɨneraɨ tells how he cleaned the place where he lives when he first settled there. He had to hunt the animals who were the masters of the place because they would bring him and his family problems and illnesses if he left them unhunted.

This kind of "cleaning up" has two components: one is to perceive and become aware of the "filth" (the problems), which manifest itself in dreams or small accidents; the other is to set up traps in the forest in which actual animals will be caught.

He says in lines 10-11: "There was filth indeed but / still one couldn't perceive it." That filth is not easily detected. A man has to prepare himself with coca and tobacco, sit down to meditate, and pay attention to his heart. The heart of the seated one becomes "a trap for bad feelings," that is, he stills his heart so that any perturbing feeling can be clearly perceived. To perceive those feelings amounts to hunting them. That is why the spirit of tobacco is called "the eye that sees, the ear that listens." When perturbing feelings are hunted in the heart, an animal will fall into the trap which has been set out in the forest.

This kind of hunting is central to the word of tobacco and coca. Whenever a person sets out on a good endeavor, Kɨneraɨ says, problems are sure to appear, either externally—as "jealous" animals or people's sorcery—or internally, as feelings of rage, discouragement, sadness, quarrels, and so forth. The prototypical good endeavor of tobacco and coca is the raising of a family, and its reflection in the ritual world is the establishment of a *maloca*[1] and the commitment to perform a set of dance rituals. When a person sets himself or herself to carry out such an endeavor, it is said that he or she has to sit down as a *buinaima,* "an

are so,

but when one doesn't know this, it seems as though *people* are
speaking against one.   185

Truly, I already
  experienced it, and
  so today
  so I relate it.

---

ancestor."[2] Kɨneraɨ says that the animals, who are the masters of this world, will make every attempt to disrupt the work of a *buinaima*. In consequence, whoever sets out on the path of the *buinaima* has to become a hunter so as to open up a place for "his children to sleep" (see line 14).[3]

What happens "inside" *(beno)*—bad feelings, accidents, problems—is reflected "outside" *(jino)* as animals. Just to set traps outside is not enough. Those feelings (animals) first have to be defeated inside. The actual hunting takes place in dreams, then an animal will go to fall into the trap outside. This way of turning feelings and dreams into animal bodies is called *monáitate,* "to make dawn." The ability to make that happen is called *dɨona máɨrie,* "tobacco power." This power is acquired through tobacco discipline, or *yetárafue.*

This text makes reference to tobacco *yetárafue* by means of three verbs: *méiñote,* "to examine"; *raɨide,* "to sit down"; and *kakáreide,* "to pay attention."

"To examine" goes together with the setting up of traps. When settling down in a new place, or a new endeavor, one has to examine things and become aware of the place. If one notices that there is danger (filth) one has to set up traps. Kɨneraɨ says (lines 20-24):

Well then, truly,
  I examined this place.
The ancients were afraid of this place,
  I truly examined it;
  then I set up traps.

In order to "truly examine" one has to mix tobacco paste with vegetable salt. This amounts to setting up traps "inside." Then, traps are set "outside," in the forest. This alerts the game—both animals and feelings. It is like declaring war; so he says in lines 25-26: "I set up traps / and put an end to it."

Then he "sits down" and "pays attention," because those animals (feelings) will come "to speak." If he is seated and paying attention, the animals will not

121

fool him. Kɨneraɨ says:

> Before it falls into the trap, the animal appears in the dreams
> of the one who set up the trap and mixed tobacco. But it
> comes in the form of a person in order to try to fool him. If
> the one who set up the trap does not allow himself to be
> fooled, the animal goes to fall into the trap.

The main body of the text is devoted to the narration of five episodes of such kinds of hunting. These episodes symbolize feelings that might arise when establishing a new family in a new place. In this text, Kɨneraɨ illustrates how he was able to defeat those feelings and turn them into forest game.

The following chart summarizes the five events:

Dream	Attitude	Trick	Game
Father	furious, holds a machete	says he blocked his path	male ocelot, caught by a foot
Old woman	sad, holds a bundle of ants	says she is the mistress of the place	giant anteater, it looks like two anteaters
Basket	impersonal	something speaks	giant armadillo
Bora woman	seductive, well dressed and painted	gets into the hammock, tickles him	female ocelot, caught by its shoulder
Compadre	friendly, has a tobacco pot	offers his tobacco paste	jaguar, caught when they were away

This chart can be read in two ways. For Kɨneraɨ, different social relations (left column) are understood as dreamlike manifestations of animal spirits, which would be the real source of the feelings associated with those relations: with his father, with different women, with his *compadre.*

One can also read the chart the other way around. It is conceivable that the hunted animals are only metaphors for the feelings associated with very real and troubling social relations. Kɨneraɨ had to resolve these feelings in order to be able to establish himself as an independent man in a new place.

Kɨneraɨ settled himself in this place after he got married for the second time, towards the end of 1960s. Before, he had lived in his father's *maloca,* next to other relatives. He had also worked as an employee of La Chorrera's boarding school for ten years, after he became a widower. Indians were afraid, for different reasons, of the place where he decided to establish his new home. As nobody had lived in that place for many years, game was likely to be abundant.

The first troubling relation he had to face was with his father, who was a powerful shaman and a proud and angry man. Kɨneraɨ hunts his father's rage in the form of that male ocelot—"It looked just like him!" (line 35). It is meaningful that the trap does not kill the ocelot at once but only catches it by a foot. Kinerai, with determination, delivers the finishing-stroke—"A tough guy?" he says before knocking it on the head with a stick (lines 50-53). He expresses his feelings toward his father—the secret competition between the two, the problems of his wife living next to her in-laws—by transposing them to the sphere of hunting.

The second type of relation he has to solve is with the grandmother, who is a source of sadness. She might represent the past, the unconscious—and a glance at the history of the last hundred years of this region shows us how sad indeed this past was. She is "the mistress of this place." That sadness is so big and its tail is so large that when it falls into the trap it seems that there are two animals.

The third episode is with a big basket. This metaphor is easy to interpret after knowing the story of the giant armadillo (text 3A). So was it for Kinerai: "But, / of course, that meant a giant armadillo" (lines 102-103), he concludes right away. The giant armadillo is also a feminine power, it represents the lazy and deceitful woman—the "unproper" woman whom one should not marry.[4] Her power is so dangerous that Kinerai refers to it in the most succinct manner. When we recorded the story of the giant armadillo, Kinerai advised me to lick a lot of tobacco before we started—"for your body to be very hot"—because by mentioning her name we would attract "that woman"—together with her powers of deceit. He simply kills her and throws her into the river.

Another female, the seductive one, also appears. She is seductive and shameless. She is not violent, like his father, she is not sad, like his grandmother,

Trap for big animals

123

she is not deceitful and lazy, like the unproper woman—she is just easy to seduce, and she keeps turning back as she walks away, in case he changes his mind. She is represented by a Bora woman—a marriageable woman, a proper basket. But she does not have *yetárafue,* she does not respect another woman's marriage. She is also killed by the trap.

Finally, the relation of godfathership—an institution derived from Catholic missionaries—is friendly and obliging, but also has hidden dangers. In the dream, it is *compadre* Mánaidiki who appears. He was a renowned shaman and sorcerer. Those ties of friendship and godfathership can be as dangerous as the jaguar. His *compadre* offers him his tobacco, which is a sign of friendship among men—and an act of hostility when refused. However, Kinerai is able to notice that his tobacco is not proper tobacco, it is not real friendship—it is just an illusion, like the glowworms that glitter in his tobacco. He used to tell me that the jaguar's tobacco is its claws, as is the *compadre's* friendship. Kinerai is on his way to La Chorrera when that jaguar falls into the trap.

That jaguar (false friendship)—or in another sense, the ties and obligations of godfathership—also manifest themselves as small and annoying accidents—cutting the hand, injuring an eye. Kinerai gets rid of them.

In the analysis that precedes I have reversed Kinerai's thought, and perhaps he would find my reasoning—that the real source of those feelings are problematical social relations, not vengeful animals—wholly unacceptable. He concludes the text by reasserting the exact opposite (lines 182-185):

> For this reason,
>   those things
>   are so,
>   but when one doesn't know this, it seems as though *people* are speaking
>   against one.

---

1 Manioc strainer
2 Manioc sieve
3 Baskets
   (a) pentagonal holes
   (b) hexagonal holes
4 Earthenware pots
5 Clay griddle

THE WORD OF TOBACCO

Bibe 4

Dɨona úai zúuiya

[I][i]

Bie úai táɨjɨe uaina ite.
Nɨɨ fui jitókome dane abɨdo
  daaje izoi mei komúikana jáaide
  jenóyena.   *jm* jm
Ie mei káɨedɨno mei   5
  ja arɨ ua ba zairítajanomo fuite.   *jm* jm
Dɨnómona dane báimɨe komo ua zairídɨmɨe dane rɨɡo uamo dano
  afénodo arɨ ba jáaide.   *jm* jm *jm* jm

Meita raa fínua
  oni afémakɨmo yogano,   *jm* jm   10
  jae biya izoi,   *jm* jm
  ja mei éikome
  fia afedo kakáreide   *jm* jm
  ua komógɨma úriya.   *jm* jm
Jae akɨ daɨi ua   15
  mooma úrite, daɨde,   *jm*
  akɨ daɨi eiño úrite.   *jm*
Ɨnokana atɨde,   *jm*
  fɨnókana atɨde,   *jm* jɨɨ
  daaje izoi,   *jm* jm   20
  daaje táɨjɨe.   *jm* jm
Meita ei izoi komuide,   *jm*
  fima dɨbene moo izoi komuide.   *jm* jm

Mei baie ja mei fuiye izoide, baie mamekɨ ja mei ua
  ja jeede,   *jm*   25
  éikome,   *jm*
  eirɨɡo.   *jm* jɨɨ
Fia ja jagɨyɨdo táɨjɨe ite,   *jm* jɨɨ
  eirɨɡomo ja jagɨyɨna ite.   *jm* jm
Mei jitókome nɨeze ia   30

Text 4
Uttering the Tobacco Word

[II][i]

This word is about work.
With this, the young people
  who are growing up
  once more seek in the same way.
Then, when they have grown up   5
  the task of the elders is done.
From then on, when those who grow up get married
  they will go forward with this teaching.

And so, when work
  has been taught to them   10
  as it was taught in ancient times
  now the old man
  only has to pay attention
  to the conversation of the new generation.
Formerly,   15
  so my father spoke, one says
  so my mother spoke.
They kept fulfilling their obligations,
  they kept working—
  the same work   20
  in the same way.
And so, the woman grows up to be like her mother,
  the man grows up to be like his father.

And those others seem now to be aged, their names are now
  old ones: 25
  the old man,
  the old woman.
Only breath is the old man's work,
  the old woman's work is only breath.
Then, who will give advice   30

yoyena,   *jm* jm
ie mio nɨeze ia yoyena.   *jm* jɨ
Aféiyɨnoɨmo ja afe dano dɨno
  ja jɨkánote,   *jm* jɨ
  moo, bie nɨɨe izóidɨno,   *jm* jm   35
  ei, bie nɨɨe izóidɨno.   *jm* jm

Mei iga íadɨ naɨ fɨgo iñega,   *jm*
  naɨ fɨgo ua daama fɨnuana onóiñede.   *jm* jm
Ie jira moo ja fɨnóraɨma-   *jm*
    -na mameide,   *jm*   40
  ei fɨnóraɨño.   *jm* jm
Mei aféiyɨnoɨ nano fueñe fɨnókana atɨka,   *jm* jɨ
  aféiyɨnoɨmo ite.   *jm* jɨ
Ie naɨ mei afedo
  ua naɨ   45
  jáaiñede.   *jm* jm
                                             [ii]

Iedo yokana éikome uite,   *jm*
  íedo eirɨgo yokana uite,   *jm* jɨ
  be daɨi nogo niga, daɨde,   *jm*
  be daɨi kɨrɨtikoɨ moi taɨneka, daɨde.   *jm*   50
Meita rɨgoza nogo niyana ja yófuega,   *jm* jm
  ja dɨnori ja iyɨko komuide.   *jm* jm

Ja
  eirɨgo
    ie jito   55
      jíibie béeɨyena nogo
        nite.   *jm* jɨ
Ie mio
  íena
    ɨkɨru nite.   *jm* jɨ   60
Ie mio
  jukuiko nite.   *jm* jm
Ie mio
  juiñoiko nite.   *jm* jm

128

to the young man?
Who will give advice to the daughter-in-law?
They will ask
  the two elders:
  "Papa, how is this done?"   35
  "Mama, how is this done?"

Although it has been given to them, they still don't fully understand it,
  they still do not know how to work by themselves.
Now then, the father is like
  the master of work,   40
  the mother as well.
They have been working all their lives,
  they understand it well.
But the children,
  still,   45
  cannot do it.
          [ii]
For that reason the old man keeps teaching,
  the old woman keeps teaching:
  "This is the way an earthenware pot is made," she says,
  "This is the way a basket is begun," he says.   50
And so, when the girl has learned to make pottery,
  from then on the chili pot appears.

Now
  the old woman
    makes a pot   55
      to toast the leaves of coca
        for her son.
For her daughter-in-law,
  she makes
    a jar to fetch water.   60
For her daughter-in-law,
  she makes a pot to cook the juice of bitter manioc.
For her daughter-in-law,
  she makes a pot to cook the juice of sweet manioc.

Ja dɨnori ie   65
  jɨfai
    ie mio
      kɨrɨgaɨ nite.   *jm* jm
Ie mio
  aidóriyɨgaɨ nite.   *jm* jm   70
Ie mio
  yókɨriyena
  yokofe nite.   *jm* jm
Ie mio
  izíriyena   75
  ranita nite.   *jm* jɨɨ

Akie izóikano
  fɨɨa yokana uite.   *jm* jm
Iedo ja jitókome taɨnede,   *jm* jɨɨ
  ua daaje izoi   *jm*   80
  arɨ moo táɨjɨe yɨɨnote.   *jm* jm
Iedo ja rɨgoza abɨna onode,   *jm*
  fɨma abɨna onode,   *jm* jm
  ja zibe nite   *jm* jm
  taɨgo fɨnoye,   *jm*   85
  yomejɨ fɨnoye,   *jm* jm
  juarɨ fɨnoye.   *jm* jm
Ie izoi eróikano ja
  ja jitókome daaje izoi,   *jm* jm
  ja nɨɨ rafue oni moo komékɨmona ie yɨɨnoga.   *jm*   90
Rɨgoza dɨbene ei komékɨmona ie ogafue   *jm* jm
  ebíruite,   *jm* jm
  ebíruite,   *jm* jm
  fɨbide.   *jm* jm
                                              [iii]
Moo izoide ei izoide   *jm*   95
  daɨnafue.   *jm* jm
Jaɨgabɨ fɨnuana onode,   *jm* jɨɨ
  juiñoi uétajana onode,   *jm* jm

130

From then on   65
  the father-in-law
    weaves a basket
      for his daughter-in-law.
For his daughter-in-law,
  he weaves a basket to harvest manioc.   70
For his daughter-in-law,
  he weaves a strainer
  to strain the manioc starch.
For his daughter-in-law,
  he weaves a sieve   75
  to sift the manioc flour.

In this manner
  it is gradually taught.
In that way, now the young man begins,
  and in the same way   80
  he learns his father's work.
In that way, now the young girl learns about life,
  learns how to live with a man;
  now she makes a griddle
  to prepare cassava bread,   85
  to prepare cassava cakes,
  to prepare cassava tamales.[1]
In a similar manner
  the young man learns the same,
  he receives that Word from his father's heart.   90
For the girl, what she gets from her mother's heart,
  she likes,
  she likes it,
  she becomes accustomed to it.

                          [iii]
"She is like her mother, he is like his father,"   95
  it is said.
She knows how to prepare the manioc starch drink,
  she knows how to cook the juice of sweet manioc,

kɨnai niyana onode,   *jm* jm
ie jɨfai jóoiyena,   *jm*   100
ie jɨfaiño jóoiyena.   *jm* jm
Jɨfai agaiye reɨe ote,   *jm* jm
ie jɨfai jiroye jaɨnoi ote.   *jm* jm   *jm* jm
Jiere komuide,   *jm* jm
  daaje izoi fima.   *jm* jm   105

Ieri éikome jiyode,   *jm*
  eirɨgo jiyode,   *jm* jm
  jaɨénikɨ jiyode.   *jm* jɨ
Nɨɨ fɨnogafue-   *jm*
  -na itɨno,   *jm* jɨ   110
  uafue daɨnano,   *jm* jm
  féeiñeite rafue   *jm* jm
  ffueriyena.   *jm* jm

Ie izóikana oni
  ñúe ua monáitakana uiga.   *jm* jɨ   115
Daaje izoi rɨgoza dɨbene,   *jm* jɨ
  oni ñúe táɨjɨena monaide.   *jm* jm
Ikɨriyafuena onóiñede,   *jm* jɨ
  gugúfuena onóiñede.   *jm* jɨ
Nɨɨ ie ikɨriya dáɨitana,   *jm* jɨ   120
  ie jɨfai juiñoina jirótate,   *jm*
    rɨgoza   *jm* jɨ
  jɨfaiño jirótate,   *jm* jɨ
  jɨfaiño ana taɨgo zota jóonete,   *jm* jɨ
  íeri kaɨmare guite,   *jm* jm   125
    jɨfaiño guite, jɨfai guite.   *jm* jɨ

                                                                    [II]

Ie izóikano jae yoga,   *jm* jɨ
  kaɨmo birui afeno mei iñede.   *jm* jɨ
Iténiadɨ ñúe kɨoide,   *jm* jɨ
  iténiadɨ kakana.   *jm* jɨ   130
Akɨ ñuera úai féeiya meino   *jm*
  iéñede uaido birui jáaidɨkaɨ,   *jm* jɨ

132

she knows how to knit a hammock,
  for her father-in-law to rest in,   100
  for her mother-in-law to rest in.
She fetches firewood to keep her father-in-law warm,
  she fetches water for her father-in-law to drink.
She grows up working,
  so does the man.   105

With that, the old man gets healed
  the old woman gets healed,
  the orphans get healed.
Such
  a fulfillment,   110
  when it is true,
  is something not to be forgotten
  and is a reason to make us glad.

Likewise,
  the man's work dawns as true things.   115
The same for the woman,
  her work dawns as true things.
She does not become angry,
  she does not become a gossip.
Instead of anger, such a woman works like this: 120
  she gives her father-in-law a drink of the juice of sweet manioc
    —the young woman—
  she gives her mother-in-law a drink of it;
  she prepares cassava bread and hands it to her mother-in-law,
  with that they eat lovingly,   125
    the mother-in-law eats, the father-in-law eats.

        [II]

Thus it was formerly taught,
  but today we do not live with such a word.
If it existed one would see it,
  if it existed one would hear it.   130
Having forgotten such a good word,
  we live today with a different word,

iéñede uaina kakádɨkaɨ,   *jm* jm
íeri meáidaitɨkaɨ.   *jm* jɨɨ

Ie mei jae akɨ dɨnori meáidaiyafue iñede,   *jm* jm   135
  uafue kaɨ daɨnano,   *jm* jm
  be yoga úrue,   *jm* jm
  yetaka jitókome,   *jm* jm
  fui ie úrue yoyɨfuena ite,   *jm* jɨɨ
  rɨɡoza yoyɨfuena ite,   *jm* jm   140
  abɨna onode.   *jm* jm
Nɨɨ jíibina úai dɨona uaido káadoga jizákuru,   *jm*
  káadoga rɨɡoza.   *jm* jm

Jae   *jm*
  akie izóikana uzútɨaɨ yote,   *jm*   145
  birui daaje uaido jíibie kaɨ dúa jira
  akɨ dɨno akie izoi kaɨ yoga.   *jm*
Buu iéñede danɨ kaɨe
  jae komuiya jíibina úriya,
  dɨona úriya.   *jm* jɨɨ   150
Jɨaɨe buu ie kaɨ oñena,
  idɨ úai mei féeiya jira
  bie izóikano mei kaɨ komédɨkaɨ,   *jm* jɨɨ
  kaɨ komédɨkaɨ.   *jm*
Nɨeze danɨ kaɨ úai féeitaitɨkaɨ,   *jm*   155
  nɨeze danɨ kaɨ taɨno kaɨ uibiri.   *jm* jɨɨ

Ie jira jaka mei ua ñuera raa
  ua fui baɨna ñúe ite íadɨ akɨ daɨi bite.   *jm* jɨɨ
Idɨ uaido mei bie kaɨ jíibie kaɨ duga íadɨ mei
  ua kakáñena,   *jm*   160
  oni monáiñede kɨóñena.   *jm*
Iadɨ mei ja frɨa uáfuena jáaite   *jm*
  kaɨ komékɨmona,
  buu komékɨñede,
  kaɨ mei nɨɨ kaɨ ua   165

134

we listen to a different word—
that is shameful for us.

Formerly, there was no reason to be ashamed,   135
    in truth we could say:
    "This is an educated child,
    a disciplined boy,
    later on, he will have teachings for his children,
    he will have teachings for his wife,   140
    he knows how to behave."
Such is a child who is watched over with the word of tobacco and
                                                      coca,
    a woman who is cared for.

Formerly,
    in this manner our grandparents taught;   145
    today, because we *mambe* coca,
    so we teach the same points.
This word is not another's, it is only ours,
    it is the word of life of coca,
    the word of life of tobacco.   150
We do not have to get it from other people.
    Although we have forgotten this proper word [we are seeking it];
    it is by virtue of this word that we became a People,
    that we became a People.
How are we going to forget our own word?   155
    How are we going to invent lies?

Well then, although good things
    will come later on, they always come slowly.
Although with this word we *mambe* our coca,
    we still do not feel anything,   160
    nothing dawns in the world, nothing is seen.
However, slowly it will become true
    because it springs from our heart,
    it does not come from another's heart,
    it is what we   165

135

afénona jitáidɨkaɨ.   *jm*
Ie jira jaka mei
  fui nɨnomo dátinide, nɨnodo mei jaka itɨkaɨ,   *jm* jɨɨ
  féeiñede kaɨ jae uzútiaɨ duga jíibie dɨona,   *jm*
  féeiñede afe úai.   *jm* jɨɨ   170

Ie jira mei
  akie izóikana ite
  mei ñuéfuemo dúuide,   *jm* jm
  ikɨrafuemo dúuiñede,   *jm* jɨɨ
  ua nɨnomo jɨaɨ baɨ batɨnomo itɨkaɨ, dátinide,   *jm* jɨɨ   175
  jaka ua kaɨ komédɨkaɨ úriya jíibina, dɨona, juzítofe, farékatofe,
                                             mazákarɨ ua,
  ie naɨédɨkaɨ.   *jm*
Nɨeze mei féeite,   *jm*
  féeiñede.   *jm* jɨɨ

Akie izóikano   180
  itɨno bie
  mei fia uaina ite, daɨna abɨna mei
  nɨno kaɨmo iya.   *jm*
Uaina iñédeniadɨ, fia uáidenia kɨóñena.   *jm* jɨɨ
Ieri ióbitɨkaɨita mei úritɨkaɨ,   *jm* jɨɨ   185
  úrue komuiya jira,
  ei nabai komuiya jira.   *jm*
Akɨ uaido jíibie kaɨ duyena
  mei dutɨkaɨ   *jm* jm
  kaɨmare,   *jm* jm   190
  iñede nɨfuena,
  fɨénide uaina iñede.   *jm* jm
Akɨ dɨnomo ñúe kaɨ komekɨ arɨ dúkɨizaɨbide.   *jm* jm

Ie jira mei
  ua, mei ua, féeireitɨkue úriyaita   195
  kue onóiñeiri,   *jm* jɨɨ
  oni ua abɨna onódɨkue.   *jm*
Iémona mei nɨno ana batɨ íteita,

really want.
So that, really, we cannot say:
  "How long must we wait?" because this is our very life.
  I do not forget the coca and tobacco that our grandparents used,
  I do not forget their word.   170

Well then,
  so it is,
  these things depend on the good Word
  these things do not depend on anger,
  we cannot say that we are going to live otherwise,   175
  because we are the People of the word of tobacco, coca, bitter man-
                      ioc, sweet manioc, peanut;
  we are the substance of that.
How can we forget?
  We cannot forget.

Things being as they are,   180
  this work
  seems to be only a conversation; but,
  where is it in us?
If it were only a matter of talk one would not see Things.
Because we feel gratified we speak,   185
  because the children have been born,
  because the mother's companion [the daughter] has been born.
With that word that is the word for *mambeing* coca
  then we *mambe* coca,
  lovingly,   190
  with no troubles,
  no harmful words.
Our heart has reached that point.

Well then,
  in truth, if I did not know   195
  I would be speaking nonsense,
  but I know about life.
That is why I say that knowledge is not in the depths

kaifo bene íteita nɨɨe mei bie énɨemo iya.   *jm* jɨɨ jɨɨ
Ua iémona oni batɨno mei taɨno uaina ite,   *jm* jɨɨ   200
  oni batɨnomo iñede.   *jm* jɨɨ
Kaɨ nano kaɨ komédɨkaɨ iyado mei afeɨe ua kaɨ uikaga.   *jm* jɨɨ
Nana ua ɨeita, oni batɨnomo ite, ó baɨ batɨno ua rafue ite, daɨde;
  iñede,   *jm* jɨɨ
  baɨna taɨno.   *jm* jɨɨ   205
Meita bie uáitajano danɨ
  ua jenódɨkaɨnia mei
  jɨáɨena íteita mei kaɨ bairi,   *jm* jɨɨ
  iñede.   *jm* jm

Iadɨ danɨ ua raana kaɨ maménoiadɨ, mei raana ite.   *jm* jɨɨ   210
Ie mei ua kaɨ jamáiruiadɨ mei
  jaka jɨaɨ afe uaina onóñedɨkaɨ.   *jm* jm
Meita fui baɨ batɨno minɨka mei urúiaɨmo yóitɨkaɨ, *jm* jɨɨ
  minɨkado urúiaɨ yétaitɨkaɨ.   *jm* jɨɨ
Ie jira jitáirede,   215
  ua ebírede.   *jm* jm
Akie izóikano
  mei ñúe kaɨ úai ite.   *jm* jm

Meita janáɨñede,   *jm* jm
  ua janáɨdɨnona iñede.   *jm* jm   220
Oni batɨ jɨáɨmɨe daaje yote,   *jm*
  jɨáɨmɨe daaje yote,   *jm*
  mei daaje ie,   *jm* jɨɨ
  daaje jɨibina úai dɨona úai.   *jm* jɨɨ
Iedo mei taɨjɨkana jáaide, íedo mei ua   225
  komúikana jáaide,   *jm* jɨɨ
  jɨibina komuide, úrue jɨaɨ komuide.   *jm* jɨɨ
Nɨno mei ua jafue kaɨ fɨnoite,   *jm* jɨɨ
  iñede.   *jm* jm

Afénona oni   230
  mei ja ua zairíkana jáaide ua jiónaikana jáaide. *jm* jɨɨ

138

nor up in the heavens, but right here on this earth.
And that is why I say that out there there are only lies,   200
  out there there is nothing.
We only care about the things with which we grew up.
Not everything is good; they will say, "there are good things else-
               where," or "out there is the true knowledge";
  but there is nothing out there,
  elsewhere there is nothing.   205
And then, despising what we have
  we look for other things,
  thinking we will find another path;
  but there isn't another path.

If we only aspire to true things, we will get those things.   210
Then, if we leave those things aside
  we will never learn the true word.
And so, later on, What are we going to teach our children?
  With what are we going to educate them?
Thus, it is something necessary   215
  and truly beautiful.
In this manner
  is our good word.

And so, we are not fooling ourselves;
  nor are these illusions.   220
Another elder will teach the same,
  another person will teach the same,
  because it is the same,
  the same word of tobacco and coca.
With this word one keeps working, with this word   225
  one keeps making things grow—
  as the coca plant grows, so our children grow.
How are we going to get discouraged?
  Nothing can discourage us.

With that word,   230
  our children will grow up and will grow old.

Ie jira ñuera ɨko bie úai daɨnano mei jae ua
  afeno imakɨ ua
  ua nɨkɨdokana atɨka. *jm* jm
Ua jino ie úrue komuiya ióbiyano   235
  éikome daɨi úrite, *jm* jɨ
  úrue ñúe komúiyari eirɨgo ióbita,
  akie uaido úrite. *jm* jm
  Urúiaɨ inɨtajano kaɨmare jíibie fɨnode,
    úhuride,   240
    zuitárakɨ. *jm*
Nɨɨ mei ua
  jɨɨrafuena itɨno. *jm* jɨ
Akie izoide. *jm* jm

COMMENTARY ON TEXT 4:
"UTTERING THE TOBACCO WORD"

The Uitoto word *zúuiya*, which I translate as "uttering," literally means "to cool down." The verb root *zuui-* denotes the transition from a compressed condition to one of expansion, from confusion to clarity, from restraint to liberation.[1] The use of this verb in the title of this text is meaningful in the context in which this speech was given.

This narrative was recorded immediately after a meeting that put an end to several weeks of discussion and disagreement within the community of which Kɨneraɨ is the cacique. The situation had come to weigh down our hearts as though it were an illness—a social illness. Once it had reached its critical point it was released as "sweat" in the form of a healing spell—the sayings of the word of tobacco and coca.

Kɨneraɨ does not mention specific situations nor does he show anger or animosity—this is a Word to cool down and heal, not to stir up disputes. However, indirect references to that situation may be found in some passages. For instance, in lines 171-174, after stating that his Word is the same Word of the grandparents, he comments:

Well then,
  so it is,

Then, they will say that this word is good
  because with this word the grandparents have
  persevered and struggled.
Rejoicing with the children that grow up   235
  the old man speaks this way;
  rejoicing with the children that grow up well
    the grandmother speaks with this word.
  She puts the children to sleep and he prepares good coca
    and begins to speak   240
    and to utter this conversation.
This same Word, truly,
  is a healing spell.
So it is.

---

  these things depend on the good Word
  these things do not depend on anger.
And in lines 188-192:
  With that word that is the word for *mambeing* coca
    then we *mambe* coca,
    lovingly,
    with no troubles,
    no harmful words.

The text is divided into two parts, which I have marked as I and II on the right margin of the page.

Part I is a continuation of the Word on Discipline or *yetárafue*. *Yetárafue,* Kɨneraɨ says, "never ends," it has to be repeated every day as it is the basis of all the other Words—of dancing rituals and of healing. That is why, in order to thwart the words of rage and discussion that were in people's hearts, he returns to the basics and goes over the foundations of behavior. These foundations, as in the Word on Discipline, start with the basic social relations: the relations of filiation (of parents and children) and the relations of alliance (of parents-in-law and daughter-in-law, in this case).

Section i of part I deals with the relations of parents and children and the succession of generations. Here, the most important point is the transmission of work skills—this is said at the very beginning of the text: "This word is about work." This succession is marked by reciprocity. Children must obey and respect their parents and grandparents, and the latter must teach and counsel the youngsters. Even when the elders "seem to be aged" (line 24), work remains in them as "breath"; that is, it becomes the experience and wisdom that are taught to youngsters. If grandparents are just "breath," parents are "masters" of work, they are the ones who actually possess the skills to carry out and teach the skills that are proper to men and to women.

In the Word on Discipline the establishing of relations of alliance was symbolized by the basket that the man weaves and gives to the woman. Here, the metaphor of establishing a new home is the chili pot (see lines 51-52). The soup of meat and chilies, which is prepared in the chili pot, is the basic foodstuff that should never be missing in a house; it thus symbolizes the woman's perseverance as a provider and nourisher.

When "the chili pot appears" the relations of alliance appear. In the commentary of the Word on Discipline (text 3) it was said that the Uitoto have a virilocal form of residence—that is, the woman goes to live next to her husband's relatives. The instruction given here refers to the behavior of a young wife in relation to her in-laws, a relation that is potentially conflictive. The young daughter-in-law's *yetárafue* orders obedience and reciprocal exchange of favors with the parents-in-law. It is her mother-in-law who elaborates the earthenware pots that she is going to need for her house, and it is the father-in-law who weaves the baskets and other basketry tools that she needs to harvest and process food.[2] Stanzas two and three of section ii refer to this (lines 53-76). With this the woman "learns how to live with a man" (line 83).

Now, as for the daughter-in-law, she has to work for her parents-in-law (lines 97-103):

> She knows how to prepare the manioc starch drink,
>> she knows how to cook the juice of sweet manioc,
>> she knows how to knit a hammock,
>> for her father-in-law to rest in,
>> for her mother-in-law to rest in.
> She fetches firewood to keep her father-in-law warm,
>> she fetches water for her father-in-law to drink.

Finally, the alchemical formula for the behavior of young girl is given in the last stanza of section iii: she has to transmute her anger into work, and the symbol of such transmutation is the juice of sweet manioc, a highly ritualized plant, the quintessence of Indian femininity. It says (lines 118-123):

> She does not become angry,
>> she does not become a gossip.
> Instead of anger, such a woman works like this:

The Father's Leaf
(Kɨneraɨ licking the tobacco paste)

Young woman grating the sweet manioc

she gives her father-in-law a drink of the juice of sweet manioc
  —the young woman—
she gives her mother-in-law a drink of it.

Relations of alliance are agreed between males and sealed with gifts of tobacco and coca, but this alliance will not be fulfilled until it is sealed with the girl's own fluid transmuted into the juice of sweet manioc.

Now then, as Kɨneraɨ says (lines 106-108):

With that, the old man gets healed
  the old woman gets healed,
  the orphans get healed.

The expression "the orphans" *(jaɨéniki)* refers to people who live with a group but who do not belong to it; they are motherless and fatherless people—not so much in a literal sense as in a social sense.[3] The reference to orphans in this text is meaningful in the social context I referred to at the beginning of this commentary. Many of the differences in the community of which Kɨneraɨ is cacique stem from the fact that there is one clan that is "proper," next to which live remnants of other clans who stand as orphans.[4]

If one examines the Uitoto version of this text, one will see that as the

144

Young woman straining the juice of sweet manioc

conversation advances the lines become longer, particularly in part II (the translation does not reflect it with precision). The length of the lines is an indication of the tempo of the conversation. In part I, where he goes over the foundations of *yetárafue,* his conversation is slow and measured; in part II, in contrast, the pauses are less frequent and the speed is noticeably higher. This change of tempo goes together with a change of focus: in part I he explains how things should be, whereas in part II he enters into the consideration of present day realities.

Part II seems to fulfill the function of validating his teachings by reference to the ancients (see lines 127-128) and confirming his authority to speak.

The person who has food-plots and has a family is the one who can speak. Kinerai says: "This word is already out there [in the food-plot] in the plant of bitter manioc, and that is the word we are talking about; we already did that work, and that is the word we are talking about"; and also: "if we speak without having a food-plot, it seems that we are speaking lies."

That is why he says (lines 180-187):

Things being as they are,
    this work
    seems to be only a conversation; but,
    where is it in us?

145

If it were only a matter of talk one would not see Things.
Because we feel gratified we speak,
   because the children have been born,
   because the mother's companion [the daughter] has been born.

And when a person gets older, when he has worked a lot and his children have already grown up, his words become mature—they are "pure breath of work." His words become spells of tobacco and coca to heal people's hearts—the same is true of a woman. That is what he refers to in the concluding stanza of the text (lines 235-244):

Rejoicing with the children that grow up
   the old man speaks this way;
   rejoicing with the children that grow up well
     the grandmother speaks with this word.
  She puts the children to sleep and he prepares good coca
    and begins to speak
    and to utter this conversation.
This same Word, truly,
  is a healing spell.
So it is.

THE WORD OF STRENGTH

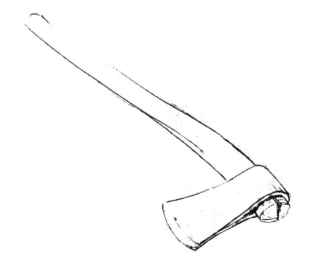

Máɨriena itɨno úai

[i]

Máɨriena itɨno
  jenode.   *jm* jm
Ie jira
  ua nɨɨe mei máɨrie uaina iya
  daɨnano   *jm*   5
  jenoka.   *jm* jm
Ie jira raa
  jetádɨmɨe jaka ua
  máɨrie jóonega.   *jm* jɨɨ
Nɨɨ máɨriena itɨno   10
  yeráberona iya,   *jm*
  máɨriena itɨno
  ɨáikoɠona iya,   *jm* jɨɨ
  jíibizomana iya.   *jm* jm

Rɨɠo dɨbene máɨriena itɨno   15
  táɨɠona iya,   *jm*
  iyɨko iya,   *jm*
  júiñoibi iya,   *jm* jm
  roziyɨ iya,   *jm*
  jɨrɨ́kojɨ iya,   *jm* jm *jm* jm   20
  nɨɨ ua máɨrie.   *jm* jm
Iedo ja maménote,   *jm* jɨɨ
  airɨ́rokɨ uáfuena ite,   *jm* jm *jm*
  amena tɨiafuena ite,   *jm* jm
  máɨriena itɨno.   *jm* jm *jm* jm   25
Nɨɨ rɨɠoza ie máɨrie dɨbene   *jm*
  aiyɨ yoina.   *jm* jm
Ie mei ɨima dɨbene máɨrie
  aiyɨ yoina.   *jm* jm

Ie jira naaga raa   30

148

On the Source of Strength

[i]

He is seeking
  the source of strength.
Well then,
  as though saying,
  "What is the true source of strength?"   5
  he is seeking.
Well then, he
  who works always
  preserves his strength.
That source of strength   10
   is in the tobacco paste,
  the source of strength
   is in the vegetable salt,
   is in the coca powder.

The source of strength, for the woman,   15
  is in the cassava bread,
  is in the chili pot,
  is in the juice of sweet manioc,
  is in the pineapple,
  is in the forest grape.   20
  That is the true strength.
With that, they resolve to work,
  they clear the bushes,
  they chop down the trees.
  That is the source of strength.   25
The strength of the woman
  we have just explained.
The strength of the man
  we have just explained.

Well then,   30

jaka fia uaido
maménoñega.   *jm* jm
Fia uaido maménoga   *jm*
féekode,   *jm* jɨ
baiñede.   *jm* jm   35
Ie jira jae jenoka,   *jm*
iya eróikana   *jm* jɨ
máɨriena ite.   *jm* jm
Ie nimánota
guiyánona ja   40
ja ua táɨjɨyena.   *jm* jɨ

Méerede rokánote,   *jm* jɨ
jiérede amena tɨede,   *jm* jm
rɨirede airɨrokɨ ote,   *jm* jm
baie mei máɨrie,   *jm* jm   45
dɨona máɨrie,   *jm*
juzítofe máɨrie,   *jm*
jíibina máɨrie,   *jm*
farékatofe máɨrie.   *jm* jɨ
Raa jetaja úai,   *jm* jm   50
fíañede,   *jm* jɨ *jm* jm
méerena jira,   *jm* jm
jetanina jira.   *jm* jm *jm jm*
Ie jirari
akɨ dáɨitana jira   *jm* jm   55
jae jenoka.   *jm* jm
Nɨɨ raa jetádɨmɨe,   *jm*
nɨɨ maɨrídɨmɨe,   *jm*
nɨɨ onódɨmɨe,   *jm* jɨ
raa fɨnuana   *jm* jɨ   60
táɨjɨana onode,   *jm* jɨ *jm jm*
rɨgoza   *jm*
fíma   *jm*
daaje izoi.   *jm* jm *jm* jm *jm* jm

                                                    [ii]
Ie jira afedo urúiaɨ jɨaɨ maɨride,   *jm* jɨ *jm* jɨ   65

150

nothing is achieved
through mere words.
What is only pursued in words
  has no weight,
  is fruitless.   35
Well then, the ancients sought
  a strength
  that had substance.
After having *mambed* coca
  and having eaten well   40
  they went to work.

They carried heavy logs,
  courageously they chopped down trees,
  energetically they cleared the bushes—
  that is strength,   45
    tobacco strength,
    bitter manioc strength,
    coca strength,
    sweet manioc strength.
The word of work   50
  is not just in words—
    because it is heavy,
    because it is difficult.
Well then, because
  it is like that   55
  they formerly sought out that word.
He who works is
  the strong one,
  the knower,
  he who knows how to do things   60
  he who knows how to work;
    the woman,
    the man
  —it is the same—

                           [ii]
Well then, with that the children also become strong,   65

jiyode,　*jm*
guiteza　*jm*
jiéruite.　*jm jɨɨ jm jɨɨ*
Nɨɨ ua moo máɨrie,　*jm jɨɨ*
eiño máɨrie.　*jm jɨɨ jm jɨɨ* 　　　　　　70
Nóoide rɨgoza,　*jm*
　nóoide jitókome,　*jm jɨɨ*
　afe emodo　*jm* jm
　máɨrie ote,　*jm jɨɨ*
　jiere komúiyena,　*jm jɨɨ jɨɨ jm* jií 　　75
　　ráiraɨe iñede,　*jm* jm
　　ñuefue　*jm*
　　uáirede.　*jm* jm
Rɨgoza komekɨ ñuera,　*jm jɨɨ*
　kaɨmárede,　*jm* jm 　　　　　　　80
　ba ie máɨrie.　*jm jɨɨ jm* jm

Nɨɨ ua máɨrie,　*jm* jm *jm jm* jm
　jujɨ raa jetade,　*jm jɨɨ*
　aféɨedo　*jm*
　jiérede,　*jm* jm 　　　　　　　　85
　　ráiraɨfuena onóñede,　*jm jɨɨ jɨɨ jm*
　　yikɨfuena onóñede.　*jm* jm *jm jm jm*
Mei jiyode,　*jm*
　ióbite,　*jm* jm
　guiteza,　*jm* jm 　　　　　　　　90
　jirode,　*jm*
　jíibie dute,　*jm*
　yera mete,　*jm jɨɨ*
　íedo　*jm*
　raiñode,　*jm jɨɨ* 　　　　　　　　95
　atɨde,　*jm* jm *jm* jm
　uáfuena jáaide.　*jm jɨɨ jm* jm *jm*

　　　　　　　　　　　　　　　　　[iii]

Akie izoide,　*jm jɨɨ jm*
　abɨdo taɨno,　*jm* jm
　nɨɨ ua máɨrie,　*jm* jm 　　　　　100

 they are healthy,
 they are courageous,
 because they eat.
That is the true strength of the father,
 the strength of the mother.   70
The girl bathes,
 the boy bathes—
 in this way
 they obtain strength,
 they become hard workers   75
  they are not lazy,
  with the good Word
  they are speaking.
The girl's heart is good,
 is full of love,   80
 that is her strength.

That is the woman's true strength,
 the work of bitter manioc,
 with that
 she works hard,   85
  she is not lazy,
  she is not impatient
And the man becomes healthy,
 becomes content
 because he eats,   90
 he drinks,
 he *mambes* coca,
 he licks tobacco paste;
 with that
 he fetches,   95
 brings home,
 finishes his labors.
                                                [iii]
So it is.
 If for some reason
 true strength is lacking,   100

moo jenoka,   *jm*
eiño jenoka,   *jm* jɨɨ
baiga.   *jm* jm
Akíedo ja urukɨ jiyótaite,   *jm*
akíedo ja urúiaɨ komekɨ zúuitaite,   *jm*   105
daɨnano.   *jm* jm jm *jm* jm *jm*
Nana ráiñede,   *jm*
akɨ dɨnómona   *jm*
afe uaido   *jm* jɨɨ
ráiñede,   *jm*   110
daɨnano.   *jm* jɨɨ
Ie iñéniadɨ   *jm*
abɨ jafueide,   *jm*
komekɨ úriñede,   *jm*
táɨnona úrite,   *jm*   115
daɨnano.   *jm* jɨɨ
Akie izoide.   *jm* jm

Iedo jofo bite   *jm* jm *jm*
reɨrúǵona itɨno,   *jm*
rao bite,   *jm* jm   120
ñotáofe bite,   *jm* jɨɨ
gurɨ́ofe bite,   *jm* jɨɨ *jm*
raa jetade,   *jm*
guite,   *jm*
maɨride,   *jm*   125
ráɨide,   *jm* jɨɨ
ɨnɨ́ñede,   *jm*
úhuride,   *jm*
jenode,   *jm* jm
monáitakana uite,   *jm* jm *jm*   130
iedo jaka guite,   *jm* jm jm *jm* jm
káadoga.   *jm* jm jm *jm*
Neemei   *jm* jm
uáfuena jáaiñeite,   *jm*
dáɨinide,   *jm* jɨɨ   135
uáfuena jáaite.   *jm* jm

 the father seeks it out,
 the mother seeks it out,
 they find it.
As though to say,
 "With this I will heal the children,   105
 with this I will relieve the children's hearts."
As though to say,
 "Nothing is working out,
 not now or later,
 because that word   110
 isn't working."
As though to say,
 "If that is missing,
 the body gets discouraged,
 the heart does not speak,   115
 it speaks lies."
So it is.

That is why he goes and brings
 firewood,
 he brings vines,   120
 brings *guarumo* fiber,[1]
 brings *bacaba* fiber;[2]
 he works,
 eats,
 he strengthens himself,   125
 he is seated,
 he does not sleep,
 he keeps speaking,
 he searches,
 he makes things dawn.   130
 With that he eats,
 he is watchful.
How can it
 not work out?
 One should not say this,   135
 it *will* work out.

Naama ua jetaka   *jm*
  máɨriedo,   *jm* jíɨ
  fia uáiñede,   *jm* jɨɨ
  ráiraɨe uáiñede,   *jm*   140
  zuufue uáiñede,   *jm*
  yikɨfue uáiñede.   *jm* jɨɨ
Neemei   *jm*
  íena jáaiñeite,   *jm*
  koko dáɨiri,   *jm*   145
  dáɨinide.   *jm* jɨɨ

Bikɨ komékɨdo,   *jm* jɨɨ
  máɨriedo,   *jm*
  jenoka,   *jm*
  baiga,   *jm*   150
  atɨka,   *jm*
  monaide,   *jm*
  nana.   *jm* jɨɨ
Ieri urúiaɨ jiyode,   *jm*
  rɨgoza jiyode,   *jm* jɨɨ   155
  nabai jiyode,   *jm* jɨɨ
  akie izoide.   *jm* jɨɨ *jm* jɨɨ jɨɨ

                                                       [iv]
Urue úriyaita,   *jm* jɨɨ
  koni éikome úriya,   *jm*
  éikome komekɨ   *jm*   160
  úriya   *jm*
  jino báɨide,   *jm* jɨɨ
  oni jenoka,   *jm*
  raa baiga.   *jm* jɨɨ
Onóiyano,   *jm*   165
  iya jira   *jm*
  yoga,   *jm* jɨɨ
  nɨeze uáfuena jáaiñeite.   *jm* jɨɨ jɨɨ
Akie izoide   *jm* jɨɨ
  nabedɨ úai   *jm*   170
  zuitaja   *jm*

It is "the master" who strives,
  with strength,
  he does not speak in vain,
  he does not speak with laziness,   140
  he does not speak with sadness,
  he does not speak with impatience.
How
  are we going to say
  it won't work out?   145
  We cannot say that.

With this heart of tobacco,
  with this strength,
  he searches,
  he finds,   150
  he brings home;
  the day dawns
  with abundance.
With that the children become healthy,
  the woman becomes healthy,   155
  the friend becomes healthy.
  So it is.

                          [iv]

It is not a child who speaks,
  it is an elder who speaks.
  The conversation   160
  from the elder's heart
  reaches to the forest,
  it searches everywhere
  and finds things.
Because he already knows,   165
  because there is a reason
  he speaks.
  How is it not going to work out?
So it is,
  the right-handed word,   170
  at the moment

157

yezika,   *jm*
jaka nɨnomo,   *jm* jɨɨ
jiyákɨmo ite.   *jm*
Iemo erókaide   *jm*   175
  úai   *jm*
  akɨ nɨɨa   *jm*
  daɨde,   *jm*
  moo komekɨ,   *jm*
  eiño komekɨ,   *jm* jɨɨ   180
  monáitate,   *jm*
  kɨona.   *jm* jɨɨ

Bie,   *jm* jɨɨ
  onide daɨnano kue oga,   *jm* jɨɨ jɨɨ
  arɨ atɨnide,   *jm* jɨɨ   185
  daama komekɨ ua kaɨmáfuemo dúuide.   *jm* jɨɨ
Meita akɨ dɨnomo zúufuena iñede,   *jm* jɨɨ
  uibíraɨaɨna iñede,   *jm* jɨɨ
  jáɨkɨna   *jm*
  eroide,   *jm* jɨɨ   190
  koni jɨfaide,   *jm* jɨɨ
  koni jenode.   *jm* jɨɨ
Akɨkɨ komékɨdo,   *jm* jɨɨ
  moo komekɨ   *jm* eiño komekɨ,   *jm*
  yezika   195
  erókaide,   *jm* jm
  urúiaɨri jɨrídote,   *jm*
  ebire   *jm*
  báɨfene
  jíyuafue,   *jm*   200
  ɨfueriya,   *jm*
  guiyáfue-   *jm* jɨɨ
    -na itɨno.   *jm* jɨɨ

Ie jira   *jm*
  onide   *jm*   205
  bie izoide,   *jm*

he utters it,
it is reaching
to the Bottom of this World.
There, the word   175
resonates—
this very same word.
He says,
heart of the Father,
heart of the Mother—   180
he makes it dawn,
it becomes visible.

This,
which seems impossible, I can do;
that which cannot be obtained   185
the heart alone with a loving word achieves.
And so here, there is no word of sadness,
there is not a lot of idle thought,
one looks
straight,   190
one gets drunk,
one searches.
When this heart
—heart of the Father, heart of the Mother—
when this heart   195
turns and looks around
the children receive
beautiful presents.
Later on
there is   200
the Word of Health,
the Word of Happiness,
the Word of Food.

Well then,
what couldn't be achieved,   205
in this manner

ja yoyɨfuena
fɨébite,   *jm*
yoyɨfuena
ite.   *jm* jɨɨ   210
Neemei   *jm*
iñede,   *jm*
koko dáɨiri.   *jm* jɨɨ
Buumo dúuiñede,   *jm*
éikomemo dúuide,   *jm*   215
nɨɨ úai raɨi,   *jm*
urúiaɨna daɨna.   *jm* jɨɨ
Akie izoide   *jm*
úai   *jm*
bie izóikana   *jm*   220
arɨ
zúuide.   *jm*

COMMENTARY ON TEXT 5:

"ON THE SOURCE OF STRENGTH"

This speech is not merely *about* strength; it is in itself *an act* that generates
strength. In "Uttering the Tobacco Word" (text 4) the tobacco word was healed;
here Kɨneraɨ invokes the power to stand up and work, to seek, to make things
dawn. In the former text he said that the word of the ancients was weak. Here
he abandons elaborate reflections and utters a conversation that goes straight
after things—not an explanation, but an invocation to generate strength.

The text proceeds in short lines intoned monotonously and marked by
continuous answers from the conversation partner, approximating the rhythm of
a litany. This succession of short lines generates a peculiar strength which is in
itself an expression of the contents. We can appreciate the usefulness of the verse
style chosen for these texts; a presentation in prose would lessen the value of the
rhythm and the power which the text invokes.

Other formal elements that characterize this text are parallelism and lists of
activities. By parallelism I mean sequences of lines with similar structures where
a single element changes. An example can be found in lines 15-21:

now remains
as a teaching,
now there are
teachings.   210
How
are we going to say
that there isn't such a word?
That nobody can do it?
The elder can do it.   215
Then, one tells the children,
"Remain silent."
So it is;
the word
in this manner   220
relieves
everything.

The source of strength, for the woman,
is in the cassava bread,
is in the chili pot,
is in the juice of sweet manioc,
is in the pineapple,
is in the forest grape.
That is the true strength.

The lists of activities also have a great power of expression. A noticeable example is found in lines 118-132:

That is why he goes and brings
firewood,
he brings vines,
brings *guarumo* fiber,
brings *bacaba* fiber;
he works,
eats,
he strengthens himself,
he is seated,
he does not sleep,

he keeps speaking,
he searches,
he makes things dawn.
With that he eats,
he is watchful.

Due to the shortness of the lines and the style of the text, the sentence syntax is sometimes difficult to interpret. This makes it essential to avoid being literal in the translation—or rather, to translate form and contents, not only contents.

Section i starts by stating the origin and source of strength—it is a matter of substance, not of words. For the man, the strength is in coca, tobacco paste, and vegetable salt; for the woman, the strength is in the cultivated plants, the juice of sweet manioc, and the chili pot—"That is the true strength." What is that strength for? To work, chiefly agricultural work, the metaphor of all work: to clear the bushes, to chop down the trees, to burn the cleared plot, to plant, to watch over what is sown, to harvest and to process food plants. From this labor food results, with that food the children grow; then there is more strength, one can grow more food, and so forth.

The strength Kɨneraɨ is talking about is substantial, it is not "air"—i.e. words. This is a key distinction in the tobacco thought. He states it clearly in the third stanza (lines 30-38):

Mixing tobacco paste with vegetable salt
(Photograph by Marta L. Torres)

162

Well then,
  nothing is achieved
  through mere words.
What is only pursued in words
  has no weight,
  is fruitless.
Well then, the ancients sought
  a strength
  that had substance.

Further ahead, he reiterates this idea (lines 50-51):

The word of work
  is not just in words—
    because it is heavy,
    because it is difficult.

The source of strength is in food; from there children will come; once there are people and food, the dance rituals can be performed. That is why the Words Kɨnerai first seeks are the Word of Food and the Word of Life.

Section ii refers to children and family. Children become well and healthy "because they eat." The first stanza of this section mentions another of the sources of strength: water and bathing—something very important for the Indians, which means much more than merely cleaning the body.[1] Bathing is closely related to the Word of Discipline. On the one hand, bathing is an everyday activity, as is the Word of Discipline; on the other hand, water is cool and invigorating, it is an antidote to laziness; besides, the *buinaima* ("the sage") is an aquatic being. Thus, the water is a metaphor and a metonym for the cool Word, the *buinaima*'s Word of life.

The source of all strength is the woman, mistress of bitter manioc; this is the root of the man's strength. With that strength the man becomes courageous, licks and *mambes,* searches, achieves, and brings home things. With the woman's strength, the man is able to search "outside" (in the forest); from the forest he brings home wood, vines, wild fruits, and game. With this the family grows.

Up to this point the text is expositive—the source of strength is explained. From this point on, the tone and intention of the text change.

Section iii poses a situation in which strength is missing, where the word does not work out and the heart gets discouraged. The first stanza poses this situation using a common rhetorical device—stating something and following it with the expression *daɨnano,* "as though to say." Kɨnerai applies this device to three complete verses, creating in this way a whole hypothetical situation with a great economy of resources. To translate the stanza with the same economy, I have used quotation marks for the hypothetical statements, preceded by the expression "as though to say."

In the second stanza he poses the question of what should be done in a situation like that—of lack of strength, of discouragement. The first verse is the list of activities I quoted above (lines 118-132). This list is not simply a succession of counsels, the very form of exposition is invigorating, it attracts the strength that is missing and that is now being recuperated.

This list of activities is a tightly-packed synthesis of the tobacco and coca *yetárafue* (discipline) for the man. It starts with the relations of alliance (lines 119-122). The man brings home firewood to feed his woman's fireplace, he brings home vines to weave baskets for his woman to harvest and process food with, he brings home *guarumo* and *bacaba* fiber to make the strainers with which his woman strains the manioc starch.

Here Kɨneraɨ refers to woman, marriage, and children by means of a double play of metaphors and metonyms: (a) to say *woman,* he says "firewood" (line 119), metonym of fire; and fire is a metaphor of woman—women are called *reɨkɨ naɨgo,* "mistresses of fire"; (b) to say *marriage,* he says "vines" (line 120), metonym of baskets; and the basket, we saw before (commentary on text 3), is the metaphor of the alliance among groups; and (c) to say *children,* he says *"guarumo* and *bacaba"* (lines 121-122), metonym of strainer and manioc starch; and manioc starch is a metaphor of mankind.[2]

When the woman has tools to work with, then there is food. That is why the man "works, eats, strengthens himself" (lines-123-125). With that strength, he "is seated" (line 126). For the Indians, "to be seated" does not merely mean to rest the body on a stool; one sits to lick tobacco, *mambe* coca, concentrate, meditate, and be watchful.[3] That is why the man "does not sleep" (line 127)— he is not lazy or sleepy, he is attentive. He "keeps speaking" (line 128), uttering the word of tobacco, as does Kɨneraɨ in text 4—reciting *yetárafue* and healing the heart of the orphans. While speaking he "searches" (line 129), as does Kɨneraɨ in text 2—gathering the Father's breath in the Mother's womb and harvesting it in the form of plants and food. Upon searching he finds, and makes those Things (game, food) dawn (line 130)—they become visible, real. As a result of these activities he is able to eat and keep watchful (lines 131-132).

A common feature in Indian oral culture is the use of rhetorical questions. In the second stanza of section iii he uses it twice:

Lines 133-136:

How can it
　not work out?
　One should not say this,
　it *will* work out.

Lines 143-146:

How
  are we going to say
  it won't work out?
  We cannot say that.

These questions have the function of strengthening and securing, of asserting that there is no doubt that following *yetárafue* one will get what one is seeking. Likewise, when he says in the third verse: "It is 'the master' who strives" (line 137), he is referring to the spirit of tobacco, "the master," because when one lives with tobacco *yetárafue,* what one seeks is already the tobacco spirit's game.

In the last stanza of section iii he states that those sought-after things have been obtained: "the day dawns / with abundance" (lines 152-153).

In section iv he no longer refers to a hypothetical situation but to the actual situation. Kinerai invokes the strength for himself. He names himself and names the power of his heart (lines 158-168):

It is not a child who speaks,
  it is an elder who speaks.
  The conversation
  from the elder's heart
  reaches to the forest,
  it searches everywhere
  and finds things.
Because he already knows,
  because there is a reason
  he speaks.
  How is it not going to work out?

Here, he uses strong words. With that word he reaches to the forest, he searches everywhere. This word is directed against the animal spirits, the bad feelings in people's hearts which isolate them from proper *yetárafue.* These are the same spirits (feelings) he hunted long before when he cleaned the place where he went to live (cf. text 3B) and the same feelings he refers to in part II of text 4. He casts those feelings into the forest, and there they turn into game; that is why he says, "and finds things" (line 164). This is confirmed by the next verse: "Because he already knows, / because there is a reason"—that is, he already knows that there are spirits of animals acting upon the people.

The following verses are the most difficult to translate in this text. He pronounces "heavy" names: *nabedɨ úai* (line 170, "right-handed word") and *jaka nɨnomo / jiyákɨmo ite* (lines 173-174). The latter expression refers to the origin of all things in the Bottom of the World (the east), where the spirit travels during tobacco intoxication. From there comes the primordial breath that forms all plants, animals, and things. When he says "heart of the Father / heart of the Mother" (lines 179-180) he is stating that those things referred to in "Seeking Out the Garden Work" (text 2)—abundance of the beginnings—are what he is pursuing.

In the following stanza he reiterates his power: "This, / which seems impossible, I can do" (lines 183-184); and he refers again to tobacco intoxication (line 191). This word of strength travels to the sources of drunkenness and, at the same time, the children receive "beautiful presents" (line 198). These presents are named as (lines 201-203):

the Word of Health,
the Word of Happiness,
the Word of Food.

As the word he used is strong and hot, he tells the children: "Remain silent" (line 217). A word like this is like causing thunder; when it thunders one tells the children to be silent because "electricity enters through their mouths and makes them sick."[4] And because it is hot—it is from the heart of the old man drunk with tobacco—upon concluding, he cools it down (lines 219-222):

The word
in this manner
relieves
everything.

THE WORD FOR COOLING DOWN

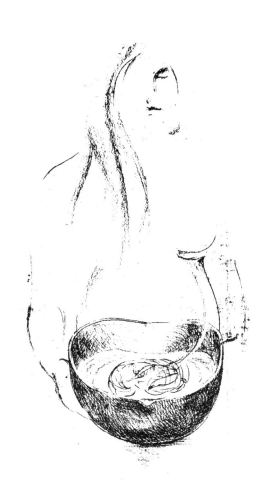

Dɨona manánaiye úai yoiye

Ie jira ja
  eiño manánaiya úai,   *jm*
  moo manánaiya úai.   *jm* jm *jm*
Ie yezika ja ua
  ja júiñoibina manánaite,   *jm* jɨ   5
  yeráberona manánaite,   *jm* jɨ
  jíibizomana manánaite,   *jm* jɨ *jm jm* jm *jm* jm
  ja ua úrue manánaite.   *jm* jɨ
Ie yezika ja biko manánaite,   *jm* jɨ
  ja ua bínɨe manánaite,   *jm* jɨ   10
  yezika   *jm* jɨ
  ja nana   *jm* jɨ *jm*
  urukɨ manánaite,   *jm* jm *jm*
  jaɨénikɨ manánaite.   *jm* jɨ *jm* jm

Ie jira   *jm*   15
  ja uzírede,   *jm* jɨ
  uzírena yezika   *jm*
  aruire úrite   *jm*
  úai,   *jm*
  dénua.   *jm* jɨ   20
Ie yezika   *jm*
  arúirede úai   *jm* jɨ
  jaka nɨnomo,   *jm* jɨ
  reɨkɨ uaina ite,   *jm* jɨ *jm*
  raa yaroka uaina ite.   *jm* jɨ   25
Yezika janáɨdeza,   *jm* jɨ
  naɨ mananai yezika   *jm*
  rairúirede.   *jm* jɨ

Ɨna jabe   *jm* jɨ
  daɨnano,   *jm*   30

Text 6
Tobacco Word on Cooling Down

Well then, now,
  the Mother's word on cooling down,
  the Father's word on cooling down.
At the moment when—truly—
  the juice of sweet manioc becomes cool,   5
  the paste of tobacco becomes cool,
  the powder of coca becomes cool,
  then the child becomes cool.
At the moment when the firmament becomes cool,[1]
  when this earth becomes cool,   10
  at that moment,
  now, all
  the people become cool,
  the orphans become cool.

Well then,   15
  they were hot;
  when they were hot
  they spoke restlessly,
  and that word
  was heard from afar.   20
At that moment,
  how many
  upsetting words there were!
  There were words of fire,
  there were words of animal anger.   25
They still are in confusion,
  they still are not calm.
  For this reason they must be corrected.

In a little while
  —so one says—   30

169

mozíñokana atɨde,   *jm* jɨɨ
fúukana atɨde,   *jm* jɨɨ
úrue jirótaye.   *jm* jɨɨ
Ie jirode,   *jm*
  úrue ɨnɨyena,   *jm* jɨɨ   35
  manaɨde jagɨyɨ,   *jm*
  zuitade,   *jm*
  nɨnomo   *jm*
  zúuijikaide,   *jm*
  biko manánaite,   *jm*   40
  bínɨe manánaite.   *jm* jɨɨ
Yezika   *jm* jɨɨ
  kaɨmare   *jm*
  aiñode,   *jm* jɨɨ
  zúuide.   *jm* jɨɨ   45
Yezika
  nɨnomo   *jm* jɨɨ
  jaka kaɨmare,   *jm* jɨɨ
  zúuide,   *jm* jɨɨ
  iya jagɨyɨ,   *jm* jɨɨ   50
  manánaiya jagɨyɨ,   *jm*
  naɨménaiya jagɨyɨ.   *jm* jɨɨ
Iena
  nɨnomo
  zúuide.   *jm* jɨɨ   55

Ie yezika
  urukɨ jiyode,   *jm* jɨɨ
  moo manánaiya   *jm*
    yezika
  urukɨ manánaite.   *jm* jɨɨ   60
Nana   *jm* jɨɨ
  dɨona komekɨ   *jm*
    manánaite,   *jm*
  jíibina komekɨ   *jm*
    manánaite,   *jm* jɨɨ   65
  farékajɨ komekɨ   *jm*

I will form it,
I will blow it
so that the child may drink.
The child drinks
  to sleep well.   35
  A calm breath
is released—
how
it bursts forth!
The firmament becomes cool,   40
this earth becomes cool.
At the same time,
  lovingly,
  the breath unravels,
  the breath relieves.   45
At the same time,
  how
  lovingly
  it relieves!
  The breath of life,   50
  the breath which cools down,
  the breath which sweetens.
How
  thoroughly
    it relieves!   55

At that moment
  the people are healed.
    At the moment
  the Father becomes cool,
  the people become cool.   60
Everything:
  the heart of tobacco
    becomes cool,
  the heart of coca
    becomes cool,   65
  the heart of sweet manioc

naɨménaite,   *jm* jɨɨ
juzítofe komekɨ   *jm*
   manánaite,
   mazákarɨ komekɨ   *jm*   70
   manánaite.   jɨɨ
Nabedɨ   *jm*
jɨɨra
zuitade,   *jm*
moo, eiño.   *jm* jɨɨ jɨɨ *jm*   75
Iékoni
   nana manánaite,   *jm* jɨɨ
   roziyɨ komekɨ   *jm*
   naɨménaite,   *jm* jɨɨ
   akie izoide   *jm* jɨɨ   80
   jɨrɨ́koyɨ komekɨ   *jm*
   naɨménaite,   *jm*
   jífikue komekɨ   *jm*
   naɨménaite,   *jm* jɨɨ
   ibina.   *jm* jm jm *jm* jm *jm* jm   85
Iékoni   *jm*
   jiyode,   *jm* jɨɨ
   nɨnomo   *jm* jɨɨ
   jae manánaiñede,   *jm* jɨɨ
   ie mei manánaite,   *jm* jɨɨ   90
   juyékori manánaite,   *jm* jɨɨ
   nogoraɨ manánaite,   *jm* jɨɨ
   zibe manánaite,   *jm* jɨɨ
   nana   *jm*
      manánaite,   95
      ñúe.   *jm* jií

Ie yezika bínɨe jírĝuenɨ,   *jm* jɨɨ
   íemo manánaite,   *jm*
   urukɨ kaɨmare nɨnomo jafírioide,   *jm* jɨɨ
   nɨnomo ɨnɨ́rioide,   *jm* jɨɨ jɨɨ   100
   komekɨ zúuide,   *jm* jɨɨ
   moo komekɨ   *jm*

  becomes sweet,
   the heart of bitter manioc
    becomes cool,
   the heart of peanut   70
    becomes cool.
A genuine
  healing spell
  is released
  by the Father and the Mother.   75
Right away
  everything becomes cool.
  The heart of pineapple
   becomes sweet,
  in that manner   80
  the heart of the forest grape
   becomes sweet,
  the heart of the sapote
   becomes sweet—
  like water.   85
Right away,
  how
  it heals!
  What was not cool before
  now is cool;   90
  the gourd becomes cool,
  the earthenware pot becomes cool,
  the clay griddle becomes cool.
  Everything
   becomes   95
    thoroughly cool.

At that moment this earth is like moist clay,
  thus, it becomes cool.
  How lovingly people become calm!
  How drowsy they become!   100
  The heart is relieved,
  the heart of the Father

zúuide,   *jm*
eiño komekɨ
zúuide.   *jm* jɨɨ   105
Ie izóikana   *jm*
manánaite,   *jm* jɨɨ
nana   *jm*
manánaite,   *jm*
dáamɨe komékɨmona   *jm* jɨɨ jɨɨ   110
jírue
jagɨyɨ   *jm*
zuitade,
rɨérue
jagɨyɨ   115
zuitade,   *jm* jɨɨ
uafue
komɨnɨ   *jm*
komuiya   *jm*
jagɨyɨ   120
zuitade.   *jm* jɨɨ
Iékoni   *jm*
nɨnomo   *jm*
manánaite,   *jm* jɨɨ
arɨ   125
monaide,   *jm* jɨɨ
arɨ
ñuéfuena
zúuide,   *jm*
arɨ ñuéfuena   130
naɨménaite.   *jm* jɨɨ

Idɨ urúkɨdɨkaɨ,   *jm*
íeri kaɨ mai nɨeze kaɨ jiyóitɨkaɨ,   *jm* jɨɨ
jíyua rafue ite.   *jm* jɨɨ
Arɨ   135
uu fuuka
manánaite,   *jm* jɨɨ
moo

is relieved,
 the heart of the Mother
  is relieved.   105
In this way
 it becomes cool,
 everything
  becomes cool.
 From the man's heart   110
  a fresh
   breath
    bursts forth,
  a dewy
   breath   115
    bursts forth,
  the true
   breath of
    the people's
     birth   120
      bursts forth.
Right away,
 how cool
  it becomes!
 Fully   125
  it dawns,
 fully
  the good Word
   is uttered,
 fully, the good Word   130
  becomes sweet.

We are the true People;
 that is why, in order to heal ourselves,
 there is a word of healing.
What is   135
 well blown
  becomes cool;
 the Father's

uieko
  manánaite,   *jm*   140
eiño
  uieko
    manánaite,   *jm jɨɨ*
manánaiya jagɨyɨ   *jm*
  zuitade.   *jm* jɨɨ   145
Ie yezika
  nɨnomo   *jm*
    bire   *jm*
      zúuide   *jm*
jagɨyɨ   150
  jiyákɨmo   *jm*
    arɨ
      zúuide,   *jm* jɨɨ
moo jagɨyɨ,   *jm*
  eiño jagɨyɨ,   *jm* jɨɨ   155
eiño rátiya,   *jm*
  moo rátiya,   *jm* jɨɨ jɨɨ
komuiya buinaima,   *jm*
  daɨna,   *jm*
moo mamekɨ,   *jm*   160
  eiño mamekɨ,   *jm*
komɨnɨiño,   *jm* jɨɨ jɨɨ
komɨnɨiño
  jagɨyɨ   *jm*
    zuitade.   *jm* jɨɨ   165

Ie yezika   *jm*
  nɨnomo   *jm*
    uákona
      jɨ̱ide.   *jm*
Ie yezika   170
  nɨnomo
    dátizaina
      izoi
        jofomo ikúrina biko jɨ̱ide.   *jm* jɨɨ

countenance
becomes cool, 140
the Mother's
countenance
becomes cool,
a cool breath
bursts forth. 145
At that moment,
how
the forest
is relieved!
The breath 150
at the Bottom of This World
is thoroughly
relieved.
Breath of the Father,
breath of the Mother, 155
seat of the Mother,
seat of the Father,
Buinaima of life,
one says,
name of the Father, 160
name of the Mother,
Mother of the people.
The breath
of the Mother of the people
bursts forth. 165

At that moment,
how
the true "house"
is conjured!
At that moment 170
—so to speak—
how,
inside the vessel,
this "house" will be conjured![2]

Nabéfuena   *jm* jɨɨ   175
    mózikaide,   *jm* jɨɨ
   nabéfuena
    jɨɨjikaide.   *jm* jɨɨ

Akie izoi   *jm* jɨɨ
    jabe urukɨ komuite,   *jm*   180
    ja moo daɨde,   *jm*
    eiño daɨde.   *jm* jɨɨ
Akie izoi
   jagɨyɨna
    kɨokaide.   *jm* jɨɨ   185
Akie izoi
   ñuéfuena
    kɨokaide.   *jm* jɨɨ jɨɨ
Ie jira nabéfuena
   moo maménua   *jm*   190
   zuitade
    komuiya
     jagɨyɨ.   *jm*
Akie izoide.

Bibe 6A

Dɨona fɨnua úai yoiye

[i]

Mei dɨona
   ua fɨnua úai
   ua afe yezika mei afeno yoga.   *jɨɨ* jm
Ua ñúe fɨnoka,   *jm* jm
   ñúe uétaga.   *jm* jm   5
Ie ja ua
   manánaitaga.   *jm* jm

Resolutely   175
   it settles down,
  resolutely
   it will be healed.

In this manner,
  soon the people will be born—   180
  now the Father already pronounced,
  the Mother already pronounced.
In this manner
  the breath
   becomes visible.   185
In this manner
  the good Word
   becomes visible.
Well then, resolutely,
  the Father's purpose   190
  releases
   the breath
    of life.
So it is.

Text 6A
Word for Preparing Tobacco

                                                         [i]
The Word
  for preparing tobacco is taught
  when a man is working on it.
But well worked,
  well cooked.[1]   5
So now,
  he cools it down.

179

Manánaitajano ja oni
  ua yeráfomo ua jóonega,   *jm* jm
  ie   10
  ja ua fakáyena.   *jm* jm

Ja dɨnori ua
  ja ɨaina
  ja ua jofo atɨka.   *jm* jm
Atɨanona ja jobaika,   *jm* jm   15
  jobáiyanona ja manánaite.   *jm* jm
Daɨi ñetá ja ua daiga.   *jm* jm
Ie yezika ja ua
  kokuide   *jm* jm
  ɨáikomo.   *jm* jm   20
Kokuide ja ua
  náaide.   *jm* jm

Ja náaide ja ua
  naɨ afe yezika uzírede.   *jm*
Ie jira ja manánaitaga.   *jm* jm   25
Manánaitajanona ja
  ua jóonega.   *jm*

Jóonianona
  ja dano
  jíibiemo ja erókaide.   *jm* jm   30
Ja jíibie atɨda ua béeɨde ua béeɨde,   *jm*
  uzírede.   *jm* jm
Uzírede ja ua béeɨka
  ja ua kaigaide,
  ja ua nɨnomo ñúe   *jm*   35
  kaɨmare ua kaigaide.   *jm* jɨi

Ie ua
  ja ua guaga.   *jm* jm
Guájanona ja
  nane meine dano   40

Once it is cool,
  he stores it in a vessel,
    so that it   10
    can be tried out later on.

After that,
  he brings home
    vegetable salt.
Once it is brought, he burns it;[2]   15
  once it is burnt, he lets it cool down.
Once that is done, he filters water through the ashes.
At the same time,
  he cooks the water
    in the salt pot.   20
He cooks it until
  it dries out.

Now it is dry—truly—
  but still, at that moment, it is hot.
Well then, he lets it cool down.   25
Once it is cool,
  he stores it.

Once the salt is ready,
  now
  he turns his attention to the coca.[3]   30
He brings coca leaves, and is toasting and toasting them;
  they get hot.
Once hot, they dry out,
  they are well toasted;
    now truly, they are all   35
    delicious and toasted.

Then,
  he pounds them.
Once they are pounded,
  he goes and burns   40

ɨmuizaɨ jobaide.   *jm* jm
Jobaida nɨnomo ja ua
  ua dúuiñeitena eroide,   *jm* jm
  ua jare kɨoide.   *jm* jm
Ie dúuide manánaite   45
  afena ja ɨmúiñoga.   *jm* jm
Ɨmúiyanona
  ja faiánote.   *jm* jm

Yezika ja ua baie ua
  yerako ero   *jm*   50
  ja ɨéredɨno ja birɨnote.   *jm* jm
Birɨnuano ja ñoráɨnote.   *jm*
Ñoráɨnuanona ja
  jíibizoma fuemo jutade.   *jm*
Jutádemo ua naɨmérede ua kaɨmárede   *jm* jɨɨ   55
  ua komekɨ zuitade,   *jm*
  jiyode.   *jm* jm
Akɨ dɨnomo
  ja ua
  ie jagɨyɨ ua   60
  manaɨde, naɨmérede.   *jm* jɨɨ
                                                       [ii]

Ja oni
  ja jɨɨrafuena
  ja fakaye
  uaina ite.   *jm* jm   65
Dɨona manánaitaja ua jíibina manánaitaja jagɨyɨ   *jm* jm
  ja jɨɨrafuena ja ua yɨɨnoga   *jm*
  komékɨmo,
  dɨona jagɨyɨ, jíibina jagɨyɨ.   *jm* jm

Iedo jizákuru   70
  ja ua uzínaia   *jm*
  afe jɨɨrado ja jɨɨka,   *jm*
  dirɨmabido fuuka.   *jm* jm
Uánona ja jizákuru nóoitaga ñúe,   *jm*

dry cecropia leaves.
He burns them all, and
  it looks as if the leaves won't stop burning,
  it looks frightful.
But they stop burning and cool down;   45
  then, he blends the ashes with the coca.
Once they are blended,
  he strains it.

Meanwhile he mixes
  the tobacco that remained at the bottom of the pot   50
  with the dry vegetable salt.[4]
Once it is mixed, he licks it.
After licking it
  he puts a little coca powder in his mouth.
In his mouth, the coca feels sweet and delicious,   55
  the heart bursts forth
  and gets healed.
At this point
  —now truly—
  his breath is   60
  cool and sweet.

                                            [ii]

Now, on the other hand,
  these words
  can be used
  as a healing spell.   65
The breath of cooling down tobacco and cooling down coca
  is received in the heart
  as a healing spell
  —breath of tobacco, breath of coca.

With that breath, if a child   70
  has fever,
  with this spell it is cured,
  by conjuring the water of the *dirímao* herb.[5]
One bathes the child in that water,

yezika jizákuru kaɨmare inɨde.   *jm* jm   75
Akɨ dɨona
  ja fɨnódɨmɨe
  komékɨmo ja ua
  jɨɨrana ja fɨébikaide.   *jm* jɨɨ

Manánaiya jɨɨra,   *jm*   80
  kaɨ komuiya jɨɨra.   *jm* jm
Akie izóikano
  ja arɨ ua yɨɨnofide.   *jm* jm
Dɨnomo ja fuite.   *jm* jm

Bibe 6B
Urue arúizifuenaiya jɨɨra

Ie jira mei ja moo
  ua dano úrue fɨmaide.   *jm* jm
Fɨmaide mei ua
  úrue abɨ rátide,   *jm* jɨɨ
  úrue káadote.   *jm* jɨɨ   5
Urue fɨbíyena
  ranita nite,   *jɨɨ*
  úrue fɨbíyena yokofe nite,   *jm* jɨɨ
  kirɨgaɨ nite,   *jm*
  kirɨtikoɨ nite,   *jm* jm   10
  nɨɨ mei úrue ua káadua.   *jm* jm
Abɨri ei
  ñekɨro móoide.   *jm* jm
Mei káadote ua
  ja ua ñúe baɨ ba jáaide.   *jm* jɨɨ   15

Benena ua jíibikoɠo kaɨmare béeɨde ua

and with that water the child sleeps well.   75
This is what the maker
   of tobacco heard
   in his heart,
   and it remained as a healing spell.

A spell to cool down,   80
   a spell of our birth.
In that manner
   this spell is received.
Here, it concludes.

Text 6B
Invocation for the Child Who Sleeps Restlessly

Well then, now, the father
   disciplines himself to take care of the child.
To thus discipline himself, then—truly—
   he sits by the child,
   he watches over the child.   5
So that the child is soothed by his work
   he weaves a manioc sieve,
   so that the child is soothed by his work, he weaves a manioc strainer,
   he weaves a basket,
   he weaves a little basket.   10
   In this way he watches over the child.
By his side, the mother
   twists *cumare* fibers.
Thus, they watch over him
   so that he will fare well later on.   15

He lovingly toasts his coca,

yerábero kaɨmare fɨnota, ñoráɨnote,   *jm* jɨɨ
ikɨ komékɨdo ua kaade.   *jm* jm
Iemo eróidemo ja ua
úrue ua dano aruire ɨnɨde.   *jm* jɨɨ   20
Ɨnɨde, ie jira, bie ua
nɨno bedáɨitana, daɨde.   *jm* jm
Daɨnánona ja ua
jáɨnoibi atɨri, daɨde,   *jm* jɨɨ
dɨrɨmabi, daɨde.   *jm* jm   25
Atɨda ja ua
ja dɨnori ja mei dano
jɨɨra fakade.   *jm* jm *jm* jm *jm* jm

Ie jira mei ua
ja fakade.   *jm* jm   30
Kaɨ mei ua
komuiya ua ikuri,   *jm* jm
ie ua rɨbei.   *jm* jm
Afeno eiño dɨrɨmaiño ibe,   *jm*
dɨrɨmabe,   *jɨɨ* jɨɨ   35
ie jagɨyɨ ja zuitade.   *jm* jm

[jɨɨra]

Eiño komuiya ikurimo
eiño rɨbei moziñokaiyanona
Iekoni eiño dɨrɨmai i-ibena
faɨribina ibina mozikaide   40

Eiño jaibikɨiño jagɨyɨna
kue mameridoɨga
Eiño rɨero buinaiño jagɨyɨna
kue mameridoɨga
Bibimo kue mameridoɨga   45
naɨmekɨi jagɨyɨ
farekai jagɨyɨna
kue mameridoɨga

he mixes his tobacco, he is licking it.
  With this heart and strength he is watchful.
Then, while he is watched over,
  the sleeping child becomes restless.   20
He sleeps that way; well then, "What
  does this mean?" he says.
Upon saying that, now truly,
  he says, "Bring some water,
  water of *dirímao,*" he says.[1]   25
They bring it,
  and then, in that water
  he tries out this invocation.

Well then,
  he tries it out.   30
"This is the
  vessel of our birth,
  truly, its amniotic fluid."
"Therein, the leaf of the Mother of *dirímao,*
  the leaf of *dirímao,*   35
  releases its breath."

[Invocation chant]

  In the Mother's vessel of life
    once the Mother's amniotic fluid is formed
  Now, the leaf of the Mother of *dirímao*
    takes form and floats in the water   40

  The breath of the Mother of *jaibikï*[2]
    I am summoning it
  The breath of the Mother of the sprinkling dew
    I am summoning it
  In this little bit of water I summon it   45
    the breath of the juice of *naimekï*[3]
    the breath of the juice of sweet manioc
    I am summoning it

187

Eiño nozeko buinaiño jagɨyɨna
  kue mameridoɨga   50
Eiño jirueiño jagɨyɨna
  kue mameridoɨga
Eiño zuuiyaiño jagɨyɨna
  kue mameridoɨga
Eiño nozeko buinaiño jagɨyɨna   55
  kue mameridoɨga
Eiño jɨfaiya buinaiño jagɨyɨna
  kue mameridoɨga
Eiño nozeko buinaiño jagɨyɨna
  kue mameridoɨga   60
  kue zuitaridoɨga

Eiño fareka buinaiño jagɨyɨna
  kue mameridoɨga
  naɨmere kue mameridoɨga
Eiño mazakaiño jagɨyɨna   65
  kue mameridoɨga
Eiño naɨmekɨiño jagɨyɨdo
  kue mameridoɨga
  manaɨ kue fuuridoɨga
  manaɨ kue naɨmeridoɨga   70

[fuuka]

The breath of the Mother of *nozekue*[3]
  I am summoning it   50
The breath of the Mother of the moist clay
  I am summoning it
The breath of the Mother of relief
  I am summoning it
The breath of the Mother of *nozekue*   55
  I am summoning it
The breath of the Mother of intoxication
  I am summoning it
The breath of the Mother of *nozekue*
  I am summoning it   60
  I am releasing it

The breath of the Mother of the sweet manioc
  I am summoning it
  sweetly I am summoning it
The breath of the Mother of peanut   65
  I am summoning it
With the breath of the Mother of *naimeki*
  I am summoning it
  peacefully, I am blowing it
  peacefully, I am sweetening it   70

[Blowing]

189

Urue arúizifuenaiya jɨɨra

This transcription only provides a bare outline of the chant and is not intended as an ethnomusicological document. The scale is E Major. The metre is free and the values of the notes are only approximate. Silences are not marked. A wider space between notes indicates the separation of musical phrases, which correspond to the lines of the transcription and the translation; the corresponding line numbers are placed in small type at the beginning of each phrase.

I am grateful to Camilo Echeverri, who did the transcription of pitch values, and to Olga L. Jiménez and Juan D. Gómez, who did that of durational values.

"TOBACCO WORD ON COOLING DOWN"
"WORD FOR PREPARING TOBACCO"
"INVOCATION FOR THE CHILD WHO SLEEPS RESTLESSLY"

The spell for cooling down, Kɨneraɨ says, "is the first spell of tobacco." All the work involving tobacco—in the garden, in the family—only prospers in conditions which are cool and fresh.

The tobacco Word on cooling down has its origin in the procedures for the preparation of coca powder, tobacco paste, and juice of sweet manioc (lines 4-8, text 6):

At the moment when—truly—
 the juice of sweet manioc becomes cool,
 the paste of tobacco becomes cool,
 the powder of coca becomes cool,
 then the child becomes cool.

All three are prepared by means of fire; for them to become useful and beneficial they have to become cool. From the images of the preparation of these substances a spell to treat the fever of a child is conceived, whose introduction I include in text 6A. In that text, he refers to the processes involved in the preparation of tobacco paste, vegetable salt, and coca powder. They involve the alternation of burning and cooling. Lines 66-73 of text 6A read:

The breath of cooling down tobacco and cooling down coca
 is received in the heart
 as a healing spell
 —breath of tobacco, breath of coca.
With that breath, if a child
 has fever,
 with this spell, it is cured,
 by conjuring the water of the *dirímao* herb.

In text 6 reference is made to the upsetting words that were in the people's hearts (see also commentary on text 4). Now, it is necessary to placate and cool down that restlessness. The second stanza reiterates the "upsetting words" that possessed the people: "words of fire, words of animal anger" (see lines 24-25, text 6). The restlessness of people is compared to a child's restless sleep. He proceeds to cure it in the same way.

That is why I have included text 6B, "Invocation for the Child Who Sleeps Restlessly." A master of dance rituals watches over his people in the same way

192

"He brings coca leaves, and is toasting and
toasting them; they get hot"

"Then, he pounds them"
(Photo by Marta L. Torres)

"Once they are pounded, he goes and burns dry cecropia leaves"

193

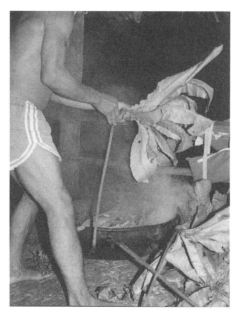 

Burning dry cecropia leaves
(photo on the left by Marta L. Torres)

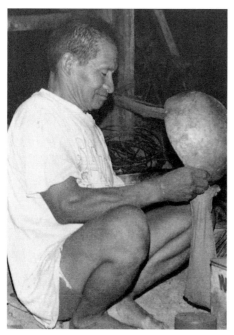 

"Then, he blends the ashes with the coca"   "Once they are blended,
                                                    he strains it"

that a father watches over a little child. He has to "discipline himself"—that is, he has to adopt a special regime of life (lines 4-5, text 6B):[1]

> he sits by the child,
> he watches over the child.

This restraint is the same discipline *(yetárafue)* of tobacco and coca. This, the third and fourth verses of text 6B (lines 6-13), sounds familiar: the father weaves a basket, a sieve, a strainer, a little basket. These references are metonyms of the whole *yetárafue*, which, in its turn, is a metaphor for the relations of filiation and alliance (see commentary on texts 3 and 3A). A father restrains himself in the same way that a ritual master must.

The father sits down and watches over the child with the strength of his tobacco and coca. But then, there comes a moment when the child does not seem to sleep well, he moans and is restless (lines 19-32, text 6B). The father then tries out the spell for the child's restlessness in a little bit of water of the *dirímao* plant. Kɨneraɨ refers to this same spell in text 6 when he says (lines 31-33):

Dirímao herb

> I will form it,
> I will blow it
> so that the child may drink.

Dirímao is one of six outstanding plants in Uitoto cosmology. These are plants that carry female powers, they are "names of the Mother"—"sweet and cool" plants. These are: *naɨmekɨ, dirímao, jaibikɨ, nozekue, katubai* and *yinakai*. Of these, I have only actually seen *dirímao* and *jaibikɨ* (basil) being cultivated.[2]

In the spell for the restless child, he returns to the very beginning of life, "the vessel of our birth." The little bit of water with *dirímao* leaves which the healer holds in his hands is compared to the mother's womb, and the child's formation is recreated with the assistance of the names of the mother:

Eiño jáibikɨiño	Mother of *jaibikɨ* (basil)
Eiño riero buinaiño	Mother of the sprinkling dew
Eiño nozeko buinaiño	Mother of *nozekue*
Eiño jírueiño	Mother of the moist clay
Eiño zúuiyaiño	Mother of relief

Eiño jɨfaiya buinaiño	Mother of intoxication
Eiño fareka buinaiño	Mother of sweet manioc
Eiño mázakaiño	Mother of peanut
Eiño náimekɨiño	Mother of *naimekɨ*

The same word he uses to refer to the mother's womb *(ikuri,* "vessel") in the invocation (text 6B) appears in text 6 when he says (lines 170-174):

At that moment
—so to speak—
how,
inside the vessel,
this "house" will be conjured!

The "house" *(biko)* that will be conjured can be "the body," or "the *maloca"* (communal house), or "the firmament" (the world's maloca). These will be conjured "inside the vessel," as the child's restlessness is traced back to its conception in the mother's womb. This obscure line in text 6 becomes more meaningful after learning the invocation in text 6B. Its metaphorical sense is announced by Kɨneraɨ when he says "—so to speak—" (line 171).

The insertion of texts 6A and 6B, both referring to healing spells for small children, is necessary to help us understand the meaning of text 6. The latter can be better understood as a spell to heal people's hearts. Unlike the spells for the child, which are sung,[3] text 6 is spoken. But, as text 5 (On the Source of Strength), it is not an exposition in prose, it is an invocation to cool down the heart and placate restlessness.

The text contains eight stanzas, each one made up of three or five verses of varying length. The longest verse contains twenty lines (lines 146-165). I have not marked sections or parts in this text.

I referred already to the first two stanzas in the first part of this commentary. In the third stanza, the drink—the water of *dirímao,* water of the Mother—upon which he casts a spell, is administered to the "child" (people). Next, he alludes to the healing power of that breath with the use of expressions such as "unravels," "bursts forth," "releases," "becomes cool." The rhythm itself of the stanza conjures the increasing power of this releasing. For instance in lines 42-49 and 53-55:

At the same time,
lovingly,
the breath unravels,
the breath relieves.
At the same time,

Maloca (communal house)

> how
> lovingly
> it relieves!
> . . .
> How
> thoroughly
> it relieves!

This power is stressed throughout the text by the recurring use of the adverb *ninomo,* which I translate as "How . . . !"

In the fourth stanza "the people become healed" (line 57). Here, all things become cool and sweet: cultivated plants and domestic tools. When he says tobacco and coca, he refers to men; when he says sweet manioc, bitter manioc, and peanut, he refers to women; when he says pineapple, forest grape, and sapote, he refers to youngsters. Further along in the text, when he mentions tools, he only refers to earthenware vessels, he does not name basketry. Those are the tools that the mother-in-law makes for the daughter-in-law. Here he alludes, in a metaphorical manner, to the relations of alliance from the woman's point of view—that is, the relations of a woman with her in-laws (see commentary on text 4).

In the fifth stanza, this earth is named as moist clay *(jírueni).* *Jírue* is an expression that is not used in everyday speech, it only appears in ritual language—it means "aquatic beings."[4] According to Kɨneraɨ, *jírueni* means "soil moistened by water," hence my translation. This line seems to refer to a primeval condition of the earth, when it was inhabited by aquatic beings. This condition is confirmed by the lines that follow which allude to quieting down and falling asleep. From this moistened earth, a "fresh breath," a "dewy breath," a "true breath of the people's birth" arises (lines 110-120). What I translate as "fresh" is *jírue;* and what I translate as "dewy" is *riérue*. The latter is also a ritual word. According to Kɨneraɨ, *riérue* means "dew, as when, at midnight, the plant of sweet manioc, the plant of tobacco, the plant of coca become cool and the leaves exude a cold and fresh dew."[5] In the third verse of this fifth stanza, the evoking power of the world's and the people's origin "fully dawns."

As the spell for the child that sleeps restlessly returned to the mother's womb, this spell for people's restlessness returned to the origin of the world. From there it is brought back to real people. Then, the sixth stanza begins by saying "We are the true People," that is, we are the people that were born from that source. And then he states, "that is why, in order to heal ourselves, / there is a word of healing" (lines 133-134). That healing is accomplished by curing the Father and the Mother, since they are the source of all offspring and cultivated plants. They are the source of true strength. In the second and third verses, there is a succession of powerful names and references. It names the Father's and Mother's countenances, which are now cool. Then, he calls upon their breath, their seat, and their names, and also names the Bottom of this World (the east), from which life arises. It concludes by naming the Mother of the People.

Once all of these powerful references have been set in their proper context, the decisive moment takes place in the seventh stanza when "this 'house'" is healed. "House" refers to "the body," "the community," or "the firmament"—or all three simultaneously. This is the metaphorical expression for the Mother of the people, whose physical expression in the culture is the *maloca* or communal house. So, in line 174, he is curing the womb of that Mother with the power of the medicinal herb, *dirímao* (see text 6B).

Finally, the eighth stanza secures the curing of this body and invokes the visible manifestation of that breath—the people that will be born.

THE HARVESTING MOTHER

Eiño ofiya úai yoiye

Dɨnomo
  eiño mei ofíraɨño,   *jm* jm
  ofíraɨño daɨna mamekɨ.   *jm* jɨɨ jɨɨ
Dánomo atɨde,   *jm* jɨɨ
  ofítate,   *jm* jɨɨ   5
  ɨraɨde,   *jm* jɨɨ
  igaɨmo.   *jm* jm jm
Eiño moniño igaɨ,   *jm* jɨɨ
  ofiragaɨ,   *jm* jɨɨ
  dɨga raa   *jm*   10
  tubúrɨna ofide,   *jm* jɨɨ
  jakáizairaina ofide,   *jm* jɨɨ
  dunágoɨna ofide,   *jm* jɨɨ jɨɨ
  jífikodona ofide,   *jm*
  jizáidona ofide,   *jm*   15
  jɨrɨkodona ofide,   *jm* jɨɨ
  ofítaraɨgo,   *jm* jɨɨ
  ɨráɨraɨgo.   *jm* jɨɨ jɨɨ jɨɨ
Dɨga raa,   *jm* jɨɨ
  urágoɨna ofide,   *jm* jɨɨ   20
  chɨkɨpírana ofide,   *jm*
  tubújɨna ofide,   *jm* jɨɨ
  jɨdokuiñoirɨna ofide,   *jm* jɨɨ jɨɨ
  uájɨna ofide.   *jm* jɨɨ

Ofíraɨño   *jm*   25
  kɨrɨgaɨ   *jm* jɨɨ
  dɨga   *jm* jɨɨ
  riga ri   *jm* jɨɨ
  riyena,   *jm* jɨɨ
  komúitaycna.   *jm* jɨɨ jɨɨ   30
Dɨga jaka jújɨna ofide,   *jm* jɨɨ

Text 7
Word on the Harvesting Mother

[I]

At this point
  the Mother is a harvester,
  her name is The Harvester.
She accumulates,
  heaps up,   5
  gathers,
  in her basket.
The basket of the Mother of Abundance
  is a harvesting basket;
  she harvests many things,   10
  she harvests *daledale,*
  she harvests yam,
  she harvests taro,
  she harvests sapote,
  she harvests inga,   15
  she harvests forest grape—
  The Heaper up of Things,
  The Gatherer.
Many things she harvests,
  she harvests white taro,   20
  she harvests arrowroot,
  she harvests *daledale,*
  she harvests sweet potato,[1]
  she harvests bitter manioc.[2]

The Harvester's   25
  basket
  has many
  seeds
  to sow,
  to grow.   30
She harvests many bitter manioc tubers,

farékajɨna ofide,   *jm jɨ jɨ*
rozíyɨna ofide,   *jm*
dɨga rozídoro   *jm* jɨ
  riyena,   *jm* jɨ   35
dánomo   *jm*
  ofítate,   *jm*
gaɨte.   *jm* jm jm jm
Jífiruɡona jifítikoɨmo ofide,   *jm*
  ie kɨrɨgaɨ   40
    moimo,   *jm* jɨ jɨ
  dɨga raa,   *jm* jm
  eiño igaɨ,   *jm*
  ofíragaɨ,   *jm*
  ofíyaiño   *jm* jɨ jɨ   45
  ie mameka.   *jm* jɨ
Mɨzédona ofide,   *jm* jɨ jɨ
mɨzéruɡona ite,   *jm* jɨ
nana   *jm*
  dánomo   *jm*   50
   gaɨte.   *jm*

Ie yezika   *jm*
  eiño ríjiya   *jm* jɨ
  riyaɨɡo,   *jm* jɨ
  mazákarɨna ríjite,   *jm* jɨ   55
  komuide,   *jm* jɨ
  jifíjɨna komuide,   *jm* jɨ
  dánomo ie gaɨga.   *jm* jɨ
Akɨ ifue   *jm* jɨ
  ofítaraɨɡo   *jm*   60
  jenóraɨɡo   *jm* jɨ
  komúitaraɨɡo.   *jm* jm
Ie izoi   *jm*
  fui   *jm*
  baɨ batɨno   *jm* jɨ   65
  úrue komuiyena,   *jm* jɨ
  úrue zairíyena,   *jm* jɨ

she harvests sweet manioc tubers,
she harvests pineapples,
many pineapples
  to plant—   35
once more
  she heaps them up,
she plants.
She harvests chili pepper seeds in a little basket.
  At the bottom   40
    of her basket
there are many things.
The Mother's basket
is a harvesting basket;
Mother of harvests,   45
  she is called.
She harvests cacao seeds,
  even the smallest seeds,
  everything,
    once more   50
      she is planting.

When
  the Mother sows,
  she is The Sower.
  She sows peanuts,   55
  it germinates,
  the chili germinates.
  Once more she is planting.
She is called
  The Heaper up of Things,   60
  The Seeker,
  The Procreator.
In this way,
  so that
  later on   65
  children will be born,
  children will grow.

úrue eróikana,   *jm* jɨɨ
rikano   *jm*
　uite,   *jm* jɨɨ　　　　　　　　　　70
nana   *jm* jɨɨ
baɨna jitai daɨnano,   *jm* jɨɨ
iedo   *jm*
eiño mamekɨ   *jm* jɨɨ
riraɨgo   *jm* jɨɨ　　　　　　　　　75
ofítaraɨgo.   *jm* jm jm
Akie izoi   *jm* jm
　nana   *jm*
　　mamékɨrede.   *jm* jɨɨ jɨɨ

Dɨnomo　　　　　　　　　　　80
　eiño
　　ja
　　　jakáizairaina   *jm*
　　　　ja komúitate,   *jm*
　　ja dunájɨna　　　　　　　85
　　　komúitate,   *jm* jɨɨ
　　ja ebire   *jm*
　　　komuide,   *jm*
　　dano ofítaraɨgo,   *jm* jɨɨ
　　aidóriraɨgo,   *jm* jɨɨ　　　　90
　　bonóriraɨgo,   *jm* jɨɨ
　　uzíriraɨgo,   *jm* jm
　　mei eiño mameka,   *jm*
　　iedo
　　　jaka ua　　　　　　　95
　　　　jɨáikɨna
　　　　　komúikana
　　　　　　jáaide.   *jm* jɨɨ
Jufáɨriraɨgo,   *jm* jɨɨ
atɨraɨgo,   *jm* jm jm　　　　　100
　magajɨ ofide.   *jm* jɨɨ
Dánomo   jɨɨ *im*
　úrue eróikana   *jm* jɨɨ jɨɨ

204

Thinking of the children,
she goes
    planting;   70
everything
may be needed later on.
That is why
the Mother is called
The Planter,   75
The Heaper up of Things.
In this way,
everything
    has a name.

At this point,   80
the Mother
    now
        grows
            yam;
now, she grows   85
    taro;
now, beautifully
    they grow—
The Great Heaper up of Things,
The Tuber Digger,   90
The Fire Kindler,
The One That Gives Warmth—
these are the Mother's names.
That is why
    things   95
        keep
            growing
                correctly.
The Great Harvester of Manioc,
    The Bringer of Things—   100
she harvests manioc dough.
Later, once more,
    thinking of the children,

jenode,   *jm* jɨɨ
riragaɨ   *jm*   105
komuiya jiyakɨ,   *jm* jm jm
ebire   *jm*
  nomédona ofide,   *jm* jɨɨ
dɨga raa   *jm* jɨɨ
eiño kɨrɨgaɨmo   *jm* jɨɨ   110
ofide,   *jm* jɨɨ
refíona   *jm* jɨɨ
ofide.   *jm* jɨɨ
Nana
  o iya dɨeze   *jm* jɨɨ   115
dánomo
  gaɨte,   *jm* jɨɨ
riyena,   *jm* jɨɨ
riraɨgo   *jm*
jieño.   120

[II]

Akie izoi   *jm*
  ite   *jm*
  úai
  féeide,   *jm*
  ie jira jenoka,   *jm* jm jm   125
  nana   *jm*
  daaje fuedo.   *jm* jɨɨ
Iékoni eiño ja
  ja jiyode.   *jm* jɨɨ
Ie izoi   *jm*   130
  fui
  uaina   *jm*
  ja ua fakáyena,   *jm* jɨɨ
  komúiyena,   *jm*
  jiyóiyena,   *jm*   135
  manánaiyena.   *jm* jɨɨ

Ja arɨ   *jm*
  uáfuena,   *jm*

she searches.
This is the root of the origin   105
of the basket of seeds.
She harvests
  abundant avocados;
many things
are harvested   110
in the Mother's basket;
she harvests
sweet potato.
Everything
  that is necessary for life,   115
  she gathers
    once more
  to plant—
The Planter,
The Hard Worker.   120

                                                  [II]

A word
  such
  as this word
  has been forgotten,
  that is why we seek it out;   125
  everything
  from the same beginning.
Thus, the Mother
  now gets healed.
In this way,   130
  so that later on
  we can use
  this word
  to grow,
  to heal,   135
  to cool down.

And,
  as a true thing,

ja eiño
kɨrɨgaɨ   *jm*   140
ifena   *jm*
ja ua
kuinaka,   *jm* jɨɨ jɨɨ
abɨ́yena,   *jm* jm jm
Nanoide   145
   úrue   *jm*
   jizákuru   *jm*
   abɨ́yena   *jm*
   jiyakɨ   *jm*
   komuide.   *jm* jɨɨ   150
Akie izoi   *jm* jɨɨ
   fuite   *jm*
   arɨ   *jm*
   uábena.   *jm*

COMMENTARY ON TEXT 7:
"WORD ON THE HARVESTING MOTHER"

In the preceding text, the power of the Word for Cooling Down conjured the Mother's womb. In the present text, the Mother's work begins. She fills her basket, and at the same time she fills herself with new life.

Throughout the text the Mother is harvesting, sowing, filling her basket. Many plants are named, and the Mother is given beautiful names:

ofíraiño	The Harvester
eiño moniño	Mother of Abundance
ofítaraɨgo	The Heaper up of Things
iráiraɨgo	The Gatherer
ofíyaiño	Mother of Harvests
riyaɨgo	The Sower
jenóraɨgo	The Seeker
komúitaraɨgo	The Procreator
rɨruɨǧo	The Planter
aidóriraɨgo	The Tuber Digger

208

so that we can carry
  the Mother's   140
  basket
  tied up
  —now truly—
  with a bark strip.
The first   145
  child
  is born,
  this is the root
  of carrying
  a child.   150
In this way
  the proper Leaf
  comes to
  a conclusion.

---

bonóriraɨgo	The Fire Kindler
uzíriraɨgo	The One That Gives Warmth
júfaɨriraɨgo	The Great Harvester of Manioc
atɨraɨgo	The Bringer of Things
jieño	The Hard Worker

The woman, Kɨneraɨ says, is "mistress of fire." That is why she receives here the titles of Fire Kindler and The One That Gives Warmth. This is an allusion to the Indian women's custom of kindling fires in their gardens to "warm up" the plants so that they grow well. In former times, women would take live coals from their kitchen stove to light fires in their food-plots; nowadays they carry matches or a gas lighter. A housewife is called *irai fue ɨgo*, "female by the stove." Women should be always kindling and maintaining the fire, Kɨneraɨ says, so that their children will grow well. When a man prepares a new tobacco paste, he stores it in vessels and places them on top of his wife's stove; this heat stops mold from forming on the tobacco paste. Likewise, if he extracts vegetable salt, he places it on top of the stove so it won't get damp. When he is going to prepare coca, he takes live coals from his wife's fire to kindle the fire to toast the coca leaves.

I have divided the text into two parts. Part I, with four stanzas of four verses each,

"She is the Sower"
(cuttings of bitter manioc)

is the main body of the text where the work of the Mother is related. These are verses that extend over several lines reciting the names of plants, and the names of the Mother and her labors—repeating them over and over again. Each stanza, however, has its own subject. In the first stanza, the Mother is gathering and heaping up—she is called The Harvester. Several of the named plants appear with the specific suffix for "seed," others with the generic name of the plant.[1] What she harvests, in this first stanza, are the seeds, cuttings, and germinated plants which will be sown.

In consequence, in the second stanza, the Harvester's basket (lines 27-30):

has many
seeds
to sow,
to grow.

She is heaping up and planting. The seeds of chili pepper, pineapple and cacao are named, and (lines 49-51):

everything,
once more
she is planting.

In the third stanza she is planting. She is now called The Sower. Lines 55-57:

"Beautifully they grow"
(young plant of bitter manioc)

she sows peanuts,
it germinates,
the chili germinates.

She is The Procreator. Sowing is the metaphor of her fertility (lines 68-70):

Thinking of the children,
she goes
planting.

In the fourth stanza everything is growing (lines 81-88):

the Mother
now
grows
yam;
now, she grows
taro;
now, beautifully
they grow.

She is then The Fire Kindler, The One That Gives Warmth. With that warmth (lines 95-98):

"The Mother's basket tied up with a bark strip,
this is the root of carrying a child"
(Photo by Diego L. Muñoz)

   things
    keep
     growing
      correctly.

Now, there is the harvest, there are tubers to dig up. She is The Tuber Digger, The Bringer of Things. She is harvesting again, she is again gathering seeds to sow. She is The Hard Worker.

These four stanzas—through recitations, names, and labor images—describe the annual cycle of horticultural work: harvesting (first stanza), gathering seeds (second stanza), sowing (third stanza), and taking care of the growing seedlings (fourth-stanza)—to return again to the harvest. Its intention, however, is not descriptive. This text, like texts 5 and 6, is a spell. Its power resides in the repetitions, lists, and names.

Part II contains two stanzas of three verses each. The first stanza suspends the

212

spell-binding rhythm of part I and refers back to the same word of the Harvesting Mother (lines 121-125):

A word
  such
  as this word
  has been forgotten,
  that is why we seek it out.

This word with which the Mother gets healed (line 129) remains in order to be used, that is, to cure—lines 134-136:

  to grow,
  to heal,
  to cool down.

The last stanza clearly establishes the analogy between the Mother's basket and her womb, which—since the basket is tied up with bark strips to make it useful—has the capacity to carry new life (lines 148-150):

  this is the root
  of carrying
  a child.

THE HARVESTING FATHER

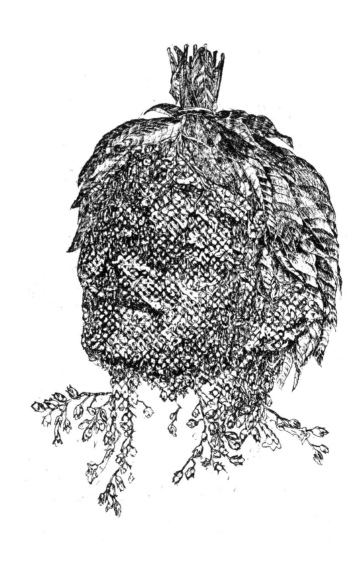

Moo ófiraɨma ofiya úai

[I]

Ua moo
  dɨbénena itɨno.   *jm* jm *jm*
Moo mei ófiraɨma   *jm*
  mameka,   *jm*
  ófiraɨma.   *jm* jm jm *jm* jm *jm*   5
Dɨójɨna   *jm*
  ofide,   *jm* jɨɨ *jm*
  jíibina   *jm*
  ofide,   *jm* jɨɨ *jm* jm
  jíibibe   *jm*   10
  ofide,   *jm*
  dabérie,   *jm* jɨɨ
    aiyo ofide.   *jm* jm *jm* jm
Moo jenode,   *jm* jɨɨ
  dánomo   *jm*   15
   atɨde,   *jm* jm
  jíibi-
   -dozina
    dɨtófede,   *jm* jm
  itófiaɨna   *jm* jɨɨ   20
  riga.
Moo dánomo   *jm* jm
  zeríyaima,   *jm* jɨɨ
  dɨona   *jm*
   zeriya   *jm*   25
    úai   *jm*
     yote,   *jm* jm
  yáiyairaɨma,   *jm* jm jm
  jútaraɨma,   *jm*
  fáiaraɨma.   *jm* jm   30

Akie   *jm*

Word on the Harvesting Father

[I]

This is
  the part of the Father.
The Father
  is called Harvester,
  The Harvester.   5
Seeds of tobacco,
    he harvests,
  plants of coca,
    he harvests,
  leaves of coca,   10
    he harvests,
  leaf by leaf,
    he harvests many.
The Father searches,
  once more   15
    he collects;
  he cuts
    stems
      of coca;
  these cuttings,   20
  he plants.
The Father, once more,
  is He Who Germinates,
  he teaches
    the word   25
      of tobacco
        germination—
  The One Who Splits,
  The One Who Broadcasts,
  The One Who Strains.[1]   30

In this

217

izoi   *jm* jm
dánomo   *jm*
gaɨte,   *jm* jɨɨ
juzíkuruna,   *jm*   35
jíibikuruna   *jm* jɨɨ
gaɨte.   *jm* jɨɨ
Dɨnomo   *jm*
moo
mamekɨ   *jm*   40
gaɨraɨma,   *jm*
ófiraɨma,   *jm* jm
ie fɨnoraɨma.   *jm* jm jm jm   *jm* jm
Moo eróikana,   *jm* jɨɨ
dano   *jm*   45
ɨaiño fɨnode,   *jm* jɨɨ
dánomo dánomo gaɨte,   *jm* jɨɨ
dánomo gaɨta,   *jm*
jobaide,   *jm* jɨɨ
dɨnori   *jm*   50
   moo mamekɨ
      ófiraɨma.   *jm* jɨɨ
Dɨnomo
moo mamekɨ
   dairaɨma,   *jm* jɨɨ   55
dairaɨma   *jm* jɨɨ
   ba ie mamekɨ,   *jm* jɨɨ
ja baite.   *jm* jɨɨ
Moo
dánomo   *jm*   60
   jobáiraɨma,   *jm* jɨɨ
dánomo gaɨte,   *jm* jɨɨ
jobáiraɨma   *jm*
manánaita,   *jm*
naɨmérede.   *jm*   65

Daibira   *jm*
   fɨnode,   *jm*

218

way,
once more,
he heaps up
little plants of manioc,   35
little plants of coca,
he heaps up plants.
At this point
  the Father's
  name is   40
  The Heaper up of Things
  The Harvester,
  The Maker.
The Father, carefully,
  once more,   45
  prepares vegetable salt,
  again and again he heaps up,
  upon heaping up,
  he burns.
  From then on   50
    the Father's name
      is The Harvester.
At this point
  the Father's name is
    He Who Filters;   55
  He Who Filters,
    that is his name.
  Now, he concludes.
The Father,
  once more,   60
    He Who Burns,
  once more, he heaps up—
  He Who Burns.
  Once cold,
  it becomes sweet.   65

He prepares
  a remedy for the eyes,[2 v]

219

moo   jɨɨ
ui daite,   *jm* jɨɨ
ui kɨóiyena,   *jm* jɨɨ   70
dánomo atɨde,   *jm*
jenode,   *jm* jɨɨ
dano baiyena,   *jm* jɨɨ
mona nɨkaɨ,   *jm* jɨɨ
naɨo nɨkaɨ   *jm* jɨɨ   75
moo fɨnode.   *jm* jɨɨ
Dáamɨe
  ófiraɨma   *jm*
  jénua
  yezika moo   80
  baite.   *jm* jɨɨ
Dɨga ijɨ   *jm*
    komuide,
  dɨga uijɨ
    fɨnode,   *jm* jɨɨ   85
  dɨga naɨraɨ
    komúiyena   *jm* jɨɨ jɨɨ
    jiyakɨ   *jm*
    jenode,
    jɨfaide.   *jm* jm   90

Ja dɨona jutaja yezika   *jm* jɨɨ
  eroide,   *jm*
  káadote,   *jm*
  fɨmáirite,   *jm*
  moo ófiraɨma   *jm*   95
  fɨmáirite.   *jm*
Ie yezika
  moo
  jaka nɨnomo
  biko jiyákɨmo   100
  ui zɨɨɨɨdɛ,   *jm*
  jefo kakaide,   *jm* jɨɨ
  dáakɨdo jenode.   *jm* jɨɨ

the Father
conjures his eyes,
so that his eyes can see.   70
   Again he collects,
he searches,
   again, he finds.
   He dreams during the day,
he dreams at night,   75
the Father dreams.
That man,
   The Harvester,
   when
he searches   80
he finds.
Many seeds
   are born,
many eyes
   he prepares,   85
the root
   for many people
   to be born,
   he seeks,
   he gets drunk.   90

When he broadcasts the tobacco seeds,
   he looks,
   he watches over,
   he disciplines himself.
   The Harvesting Father   95
   disciplines himself.
At that moment
   the Father,
   how,
   in the Bottom of this World,   100
   he relieves his eye!
His ear listens,
   his heart seeks.

221

Moo komekɨ   *jm*
  uakɨ,   *jm* jɨɨ   105
  yonérakɨ,   *jm*
  jafíraikɨ,   *jm*
  zegóraikɨ,   *jm* jɨɨ
  zuitáraikɨ.   *jm* jm jm

Fɨnode   *jm*   110
  nabéfuena,
  riárokɨ komuiya   *jm*
  jiyakɨ   *jm*
  erókaide.   *jm*
Ie izoi   *jm*   115
  fui
  urukɨ komuite,   *jm*
  jizákuru komuite,   *jm*
  ikɨ komuite   *jm*
  daɨnano.   *jm*   120
Dánomo   *jm*
  moo
  fɨnode   *jm*
  ófiraɨma   *jm*
  úriya   125
  úai.   *jm* jm

                    [II]

Akie izoi   *jm* jm
  neemei kaɨ komúiñeite,   *jm* jɨɨ
  neemei kaɨ
    raana itɨno   *jm*   130
    féeide,   *jm*
  koko dáɨiri,   *jm*
  féeiñede.   *jm* jɨɨ
Eiño ofíraɨño dánomo gaɨte,   *jm*
  moo ófiraɨma dánomo gaɨte,   *jm* jɨɨ   135
  urukɨ komuiya jiyakɨ   *jm*
  taɨnede.   *jm* jɨɨ
Neemei

Heart of the Father,
  True Heart,   105
  Heart of the Ancients,
  Heart of the Beginning of the World,
  Heart of Healing,
  Free Heart.

He works   110
  resolutely;
  he turns his attention
  to the root
  of the origin of cultivated plants.
In this way,   115
  later on,
  the people will multiply,
  the children will multiply,
  this heart will grow,
  so to speak.   120
Once more
  the Father
  prepares
  the word of
  The Harvester's   125
  conversation.

                                       [II]

In this way,
  How can we not multiply?
  How can we say
    that our things   130
    have been forgotten?
  We can not say that;
  they have not been forgotten.
The Harvesting Mother again is heaping up,
  The Harvesting Father again is heaping up,   135
  the root of the origin of the people
  is beginning.
How are we

afeno   *jm*
fɨébite,   *jm*   140
kaɨ dáɨiri,   *jm*
fɨébiñede.   *jm* jɨ

Iedo
moo
  nana   145
   mamékɨna
    onode,   *jm*
  eiño
   ofíraɨño   *jm*
    onode,   *jm* jɨ   150
  fɨnuana,   *jm* jɨ
   komúitajana   *jm*
    onode.   *jm* jɨ
Ie izoi   *jm*
  arɨ   155
  jizákuru kaɨ komúitate   *jm*
  uaina
  ja
  fɨébite,   *jm*
  ñúe   160
  arɨ   *jm*
  monaide.
Akɨ dɨnori
  fuite   *jm*
  ibena.   *jm*   165

going to say
that it   140
was discarded?
It was not discarded.

Hence,
　the Father
　　knows   145
　　　all
　　　　the names;
　the Mother,
　　The Harvester,
　　　knows;   150
　she knows
　　how to work,
　　　how to make things multiply.
In this way,
　the word   155
　to make
　our children grow
　still
　remains.
　It dawns   160
　fully
　and well.
At this point,
　this Leaf
　concludes.   165

Jifíkona ui daiya
iémona komuide ziera ikaki

Jae fueñe
  kue ua
  jitókomena
  zairiya
  fakaize.   5
Mei ráfuena onóiñedikue,   *jii*
  fia ua imaki yuaina   *jii*
  fia kakádikue.
Iemo
  mei ua fia ua onoiga ráfueita,   10
  raire kue onori.   *jii*
Ie jira mei
  jitókome ui daite.   *jii*

Ie jira aféie mánue mameki mei
  jifíkona,   *jii*   15
  íena ja kue ui daitikue.   *jii*
Daiyánona
  ja fimáidikue,
  ua ñúe fimaika,   *jii*
  ua daa fivui ua fiide.   *jii*   20
Mei táinomo kome ua izi kakade
  ie jira fimaika.   *jii*
Ie jira
  ziaiki riñega,
  jífikoyi yiñega,   25
  jirikue yiñega,
  roziyi yiñega,
  ainírite riñega,
  mairide riñega,
  rigo uieko mei eróiñede,   30

A Story About Conjuring the Eyes
And Problems Resulting from That

This happened
  a long time ago
  when I
  was still
  a young boy.   5
But, I did not have any knowledge,
  I only heard
  what the elders told.
Because
  knowledge is not acquired so easily   10
  that I could have known that quickly.
Well then,
  as a boy, I conjured my eyes.

Well then, the name of that remedy is
  jifíkona;   15
  with that remedy, I conjured my eyes.[1]
After conjuring my eyes
  I disciplined myself;
  truly I was well disciplined,
  for a month I curbed myself.   20
Because one feels pain in vain
  if one does not discipline oneself.[2]
Well then,
  one does not eat grubs,
  one does not taste sapote   25
  one does not taste forest grape,
  one does not taste pineapple,
  one does not eat animals that bite,
  one does not eat fierce animals,
  one does look at women's faces,   30

227

mei ui rairuide. *jɨ*

Ie baɨmo
ja ua
ui fakátate, *jɨ*
dama kome úrue 35
ɨrátaiya yezika, *jɨ* jm
kome aɨ ɨrátaiya yezika, *jɨ*
kome mirɨgo ɨrátaiya yezika, *jɨ*
kome aama ɨrátaiya yezika. *jɨ*
Afe abɨ rátide, *jɨ* 40
ɨráfuena itínona kɨóiyena, *jɨ* jm
jenúizaɨna itɨno kɨóiyena,
ikírafuena itɨno kɨóiyena,
ie jira rátide. *jɨ* jm

Ie jira ja 45
kue ui daiya yezika
daa enókaizaɨ ie, *jɨ*
akɨ kue ñekore, *jɨ*
dúkɨide, *jɨ*
imani ja abímona bite, *jɨ* 50
ie mamekɨ Aniva. *jɨ*
Ie jira kue, jɨfai, kue jɨaɨ kue ui
dai, daɨde. *jɨ* jm
Ie jira
kue daɨdɨkue, mei ñeko bie 55
jɨaɨe mánue jetáñedɨmɨemona fɨgora, *jɨ*
ie mei jɨaɨe mánue jetádɨmɨemo fɨénide, *jɨ*
daɨdɨkue.
Ie jira
jetáñedɨkue, daɨde, 60
ua minɨkana jetáñedɨkue, daɨde.

Ie jira
aa, daɨdɨkue,
atɨ mei koko daiyɨ.

but one takes care of the eyes.

Afterwards,
  truly,
  one tests the eyes.
  But only when   35
    one's child is ill,
  when one's wife is ill,
  when one's sister is ill,
  when one's brother is ill.
Then one sits down   40
  to see the illnesses that there are,
  to see the filth that there is,
  to see the anger that there is.
  For those reasons one is seated

Well then,   45
  when I had conjured my eyes,
  one man of the *enókaizai* clan,[3]
  whom I call son-in-law,
  arrived.
  He came from the big river,[4]   50
  his name is Aníbal.
Well then, "Conjure my eyes too,
  father-in-law," he said.
Then,
  I said, "Well, son-in-law, this   55
  is good for one who has not tried another remedy,
  but is bad for one who has tried another remedy,"
  I told him.
Well then,
  "I haven't tried anything!" he said,   60
  "truly, I haven't tried anything," he said.

Well then,
  "Ah!" I said,
  "Come here, I'll conjure you."

229

Ie jira afémɨe ui ja   65
  kue daitaka. *jɨ* jm
Ie jira
  daa fɨvui o fɨmairi, daɨdɨkue. *jɨ*
Ie jira jii daɨde.
Ie daiyánona   70
  ja bene Nofɨkomo jáaide. *jɨ*

Nofɨkomona meine jáaide, *jɨ*
  kaɨ iyánomo dúkɨide,
  afémɨe ui
  ja ua   75
  ua tekáikaide, *jɨ* jm
  ua duere zefuide. jm
Ie jira
  nɨeze ítɨo, daɨdɨkue.
Ja kue ui fíakade, daɨde.   80
Uafue, daɨdɨkue.

Ie kaɨ
  éikome ite íadɨ, *jɨ*
  ja ua nɨeze dátɨñede. *jɨ*
Ie jira kue daɨdɨkue, moo,   85
  ñekore ui izírede. *jɨ*
Ie jira mooma kuena daɨde,
  jadie kaɨ jíibie béeɨdeita
  kaɨ eroiri, daɨde,
  jíibiena béeɨñede.   90
Ie jira kue daɨdɨkue,
  aa, daɨdɨkue.

Ie jíibie fɨnódɨkaɨ ja ua,
  fuitɨkaɨ. *jɨ*
Iemo kakáreidɨkue   95
  ua zuaire éede. *jɨ*
Ie jira afémɨe uáidotɨkue, *jɨ*
  ñeko, bi, daɨdɨkue. *jɨ* jm

Well then, I conjured 65
  his eyes.
Well then,
  "You have to discipline yourself for a month," I said.
Well then, "Yes," he said.
After I conjured him, 70
  he left and went to La Chorrera.

Upon his return from La Chorrera,
  he arrived at our house.
  His eyes,
  now truly, 75
  were upside down,
  he was suffering a lot.
Well then,
  "What's happened to you?" I asked him.
"My eyes are ruined," he said. 80
"Is that so?" I said.

And because
  our elder was still alive,
  how could I not tell him?
Well then, I said, "Papa, 85
  my son-in-law's eyes are hurting him."
Well then, my father said to me,
  "Does that gentleman, by chance, toast our coca?
  Why should we worry about him?
  He does not toast our coca." 90
Then, I said,
  "Ah!" I said.

We were preparing our coca,
  and we had already finished.
I was watchful, with the coca; 95
  he was crying out in pain.
Well then, I called him,
  "Son-in-law, come here," I said.

Ie jira bite.

Nɨeze ítɨo, daɨdɨkue. *jɨɨ*   100
Ja kue ui
  ua ja fíakade, daɨde.
Mɨnɨka jetádɨo;
  kue jetáñedɨkue . . . jetádɨo,
  kue dɨnena daɨdɨkue.   105
Ie ñetá meine
  janókaidɨkue, *jɨɨ*
  ja meine kue oga *jɨɨ*
  jifíkona iyɨno. *jɨɨ* jɨɨ

Ie ñetá   110
  mai o ɨnɨai, daɨdɨkue,
  ɨna fui
  mɨnɨkana kue kɨóia *jɨɨ*
  fui o yóitɨkue, daɨdɨkue. *jɨɨ*
Ie jira afémɨe ɨnɨaide,   115
  ua tɨɨ ñéfikaide, *jɨɨ*
  manánaite ua ɨnɨde. *jɨɨ* jɨɨ
Ie meino kue ua kakáreidɨkue, *jɨɨ*
  ua kakáreidɨkue.
Ua daɨi kue abɨ manánaiyamona   120
  ja kue komekɨ ua ɨnɨbikaide. *jɨɨ*

Ɨnɨbikaidɨkue,
  ua ja bite *jɨɨ*
  ua biko erodo ua féekano ua bite ua kue nɨkɨdote,
  ua kue zaitákaide.   125
Erókaidɨkue be,
  ua kue
  ua onoɨdo ua janáoɨtɨkue, *jɨɨ*
  kue janáoɨa ua
  ja ie daɨi daɨi daɨi,   130
  baie izoi jáaide daɨi,
  ua bátɨde monáizaide. *jɨɨ* jm

Well then, he came.

"How are you?" I said.   100
"My eyes
   are now ruined," he said.
"What remedy did you use?"
   "I did not use any remedy . . . " "You *did* use one!"
   I told him.   105
After that, I began
   to have doubts,
   and I decided to withdraw the power of
   the *jifíkona* I had placed on his eyes.[7]

Once that was done,   110
   I said, "Now, go to sleep,
   in a while,
   if I see anything
   I'll tell you later," I said.
Well then, he went to sleep,   115
   and he became silent,
   he slept calmly.
After that, I was watchful,
   truly, I was watchful.
And so, when my body cooled down   120
   my heart started to fall asleep.

I was falling asleep
   when something came . . .
   Something came flying over the top of the house, it came after me,
   it tried to catch me.   125
I turned to look, "There it is!"
   and I
   scared it away with my hand;
   after scaring it away,
   now this thing—like this, like this, like this—   130
   now it was flying like that,
   and went over there to dawn.

Ie jira
  aa, daɨdɨkue,
  ɨko ite, daɨdɨkue; *jɨɨ* jm   135
  ie kue ja kaziya. *jɨɨ*
Kazídɨkue, ɨko
  nɨkáɨritɨkue, *jɨɨ*
  daɨdɨkue,
  ua nɨeze ua dáɨitade. *jɨɨ*   140

Komekɨ ua uibidɨkue, *jɨɨ*
  íemo ja ua monáidɨkaɨ.
Ja ua monáidɨkaɨ
  ja kue fákuaɨbidɨkue *jɨɨ*
  joraimo. *jɨɨ*   145
Dɨno fáko-fákodɨkue, *jɨɨ*
  ua fákodɨkue,
  ua jáɨkɨri ia. *jɨɨ*
Nɨnena afe nuikɨ ja ua mei monari
  ja afe nuikɨ ua féekano bite, ua bite, eróidɨkue;   150
  afe núikɨdo eróidɨkue, ua eróidɨkue,
  ua daɨi ana bite ua
  kaifona ua
  ua jorai dáfenemo
  ua ba chamu ie zaitáfɨrena izoi ua   155
  zaitade. *jɨɨ*

Ie jira jáaidɨkuemo
  ua kaifo féekano kue jáaiye daɨna abɨna
  ja fia dɨno iaiko bute ie
  jáɨnoibi. *jɨɨ*   160
Fia oni ja bite kue dɨne,
  fɨkano bite,
  ua fɨkano bite, bite, bita,
  ja kue ja ua fákuadado
  raiñode kaifo *canoa* ero kue bɨtaka. *jɨɨ*   165
Ie jira meine bitɨkue jofomo,
  kue atɨka afe jofomo. *jɨɨ*

Well then,
  "Ah!" I said,
  "So, there is something!" I said,   135
  and then I woke up.
I woke up, "This is
  what I dreamt,"
  I said,
  "What does it mean?"   140

I was remembering the dream
  when the day broke.
Now, the day broke,
  and I went to the lake
  to fish.   145
There, I was fishing and fishing.
  I was fishing
  until noon.
I don't know where that hawk came from.
  Now, that hawk came flying—it came—I was looking at it;   150
  I was looking and looking at that hawk,
  when it came straight down
  from the sky
  to the middle of the lake,
  as they usually do to catch fish,   155
  and it caught one!

Well then, when I was just about to leave,
  the hawk that flew down when I was about to go
  broke its wing
  upon hitting the water.   160
It came just to where I was,
  it came swimming.
  It came swimming, swimming, and reached me;
  and I, with my fishing pole,
  caught it and threw it into the canoe.   165
Well then, I went back to the house
  and brought it with me.

Ie jira
  afémɨe uáidotɨkue,   *jɨ*
  be o uimo daɨi komuide,   *jɨ jɨ*   170
  afémɨena daɨdɨkue.
O ɨko bie nuikɨ mánuena o jetádɨo,   *jɨ*
  afémɨena daɨdɨkue.   *jɨ*
Ie jira, jɨ, daɨde,
  imani abɨ namakɨ, daɨde,   *jɨ*   175
  jitókomɨnɨ
  chamu dúkɨiyena
  nuikɨ ui daitɨmakɨ, daɨde,
  ie jira kue aféɨe kɨgɨdo
  kue jɨaɨ dáaitɨkue, daɨdɨkue,   180
  ie jira kue ui afémakɨ daite.   *jɨ*
Aa, daɨdɨkue,
  nɨbái mei o jáanoga,   *jɨ*
  ie jira ja nia o ui fiide,   *jɨ*
  daɨdɨkue.   185
Ja mei benómona o mei ua
  fia ja ite o raana o ñéitɨo,   *jɨ*
  akɨ daɨi afémɨena daɨdɨkue.   *jɨ*

COMMENTARY ON TEXTS 8 AND 8A:

"WORD ON THE HARVESTING FATHER"
"A STORY ABOUT CONJURING THE EYES
AND PROBLEMS RESULTING FROM THAT"

The work of the Harvesting Mother is about manioc, tubers and fruits. The work of the Harvesting Father, by contrast, begins with tobacco and coca.

The coca is propagated from stem cuttings, while the tobacco is sown from seeds. The tobacco seeds grow in small seed-capsules which one has to split open; then, one strains them in order to separate the seed-pod from the seeds, and finally these small seeds—about 1/50" in diameter—are broadcast over the

Well then,
  I called my son-in-law,
  "This is what damaged your eyes," 170
  I told him.
"You, then, used the remedy of this hawk,"
  I told him.
Well then, "Yes," he said,
  "the people from the big river," he said, 175
  "the boys,
  in order to catch fish,
  conjure their eyes with hawk's magic," he said.
  "Well then, I, living in their midst,
  I told them to give it to me as well; 180
  well then, they conjured me."
"Ah!" I said,
  "Why did you lie to me?
  for that reason you almost ruined your eyes,"
  I said. 185
"From now on,
  that power will be useless to you,"
  in this way I told him.

Flowers of tobacco

Seeds of tobacco

garden. For this reason, the Father receives the titles of The One Who Splits (the seed-pods), The One Who Strains (the seeds out of the pods), and The One Who Broadcasts (the little seeds in the garden).

In the second stanza the Father is planting. Here, he is called The Heaper Up of Things, The Harvester, The Maker. The three last verses of the second stanza (lines 44-65) refer to the preparation of vegetable salt. In the first verse (lines 44-52), the Father is heaping up vegetable material and burning it.[1] The next verse (lines 53-58) alludes to the filtering of water through the ashes to precipitate the salts—the Father is called He Who Filters. In the third verse (lines 59-65) the Father is called He Who Burns; here, reference is made to the boiling of the liquid that results from the filtering. Once it is boiled, one lets it cool down and "Once cold / it becomes sweet" (lines 64-65). Compare this description to the one in text 6A, lines 12-27 and-58-61.

The vegetable salt is mixed with the tobacco paste. This is one of the weapons of the tobacco hunter. With the vegetable salt, Kɨnerai says, one kills game. That is why, in the next stanza, the Father conjures his eyes. To conjure the eyes means to acquire the power to uncover what is hidden: illnesses, "filth" (animal anger), problems (human anger). This power is obtained through tobacco and coca *yetárafue* (discipline): to work, to sit down, to be watchful. This power, however, can also be increased by the use of certain plants, so long as they are properly administered—that is, following the appropriate restrictions.

To illustrate this, I have included text 8A, in which Kɨnerai tells how he conjured his eyes when he was young with the plant called *jifíkona*.[2] This magical power for the eyes is used (lines 35-44, text 8A):

238

But only when
   one's child is ill,
when one's wife is ill,
when one's sister is ill,
  when one's brother is ill.
 Then one sits down,
   to see the illnesses that there are,
   to see the filth that there is,
   to see the anger that there is.
For those reasons one is seated.

Text 8A illustrates the importance of using that kind of plant—"power" plants—properly, that is, to discipline oneself and not mix them with other powers—animal powers in this case. Kinerai's own eyes, which had already been conjured, allowed him to discover, in a dream vision, the source of his son-in-law Aníbal's problem. In that vision, he strikes an animal spirit, and the next day a hawk breaks its wing when diving for a fish in the lake—a very rare thing for a hawk. This happened, Kinerai explains, because the spirit of the animal had been already struck in the dream; then it went to dawn in the lake.

The restrictions associated with the conjuration of the eyes prescribe two kinds of things: contact with sweet things, including women, and with animals that bite or are fierce. The two prohibitions allude to a delicate balance. Sweetness distracts the eye, so that one concentrates upon non-essential things—therefore, making visions unreliable. While fierceness can damage the eye, as was the case with Anibal, who had previously conjured his eyes with the power of the hawk, a fierce animal, and almost ruined his eyes.

With his eyes conjured the Father is watchful, searches, pays attention, and becomes intoxicated. If the agricultural work and the growth of plants is the image of the Mother's fecundity, for the Father the germinating seeds are likened to eyes that search and find. Kinerai says, in text 8 (lines 82-90):

Many seeds
   are born,
many eyes
   he prepares,
the root
   for many people
   to be born,
   he seeks,
   he gets drunk.

The seed that germinates is the image of the eye that discovers. That is why the

"He cuts stems of coca"   "These cuttings he plants"

restrictions on tobacco seed planting are comparable to the restrictions on conjuring the eye. We already saw, in text 8A, the kind of restrictions associated with the use of the *jifíkona* plant. Likewise, when a man sows tobacco seeds he has to follow certain restrictions: he should not eat fat or sweets and refrain from rage, among others. He refers to these restrictions in the first verse of the fourth stanza (lines 91-96):

> When he broadcasts the tobacco seeds,
> > he looks,
> > he watches over,
> > he disciplines himself.
> > The Harvesting Father
> > disciplines himself.

The Father gets drunk and searches for the root from which the people are born—the Bottom of this World where all cultivated plants and wild game come from. There (lines 99-103),

> > how,
> > in the Bottom of this World,
> > he relieves his eye!
> > His ear listens,
> > his heart seeks.

240

The heart of the intoxicated Father then receives beautiful names:

moo komeki	Heart of the Father
uaki	True Heart
yoneraki	Heart of the Ancients[3]
jafiraiki	Heart of the Beginning of the World[4]
zegoraiki	Heart of Healing
zuitaraiki	Free Heart

In the fifth stanza, he explains what the Father is seeking and why he speaks this way: to multiply the people, to multiply the children (see lines 115-126).

These five stanzas form what I have marked as part I, which is "the conversation of The Harvester." Part II is a reflection and a conclusion. Here, Kinerai conjures the Father and Mother's heart and, with an inspiring optimism, states (lines 134-142):

The Harvesting Mother again is heaping up,
   the Harvesting Father again is heaping up,
   the root of the origin of the people
   is beginning.
How are we
   going to say
   that it
   was discarded?
   It was not discarded.

241

THE TRUE MAN AND WOMAN

Dɨona uaido jíibina uaido
arɨ kaɨ mózizaɨbiya úai yoina

[i]

Ie jira mei bie
  izoide   *jm* jɨɨ
  mei ñuefue ua ite íadɨ   *jm* jm
  mei buinaima komékɨmo ite.   *jm* jm
Ie nɨeze eróikano mei ua óitɨkaɨ.   *jm* jm   5
Ie jira buináimamo ite daɨna jira ua
  ja ua ñúe dɨona fɨnódɨmɨe,   *jm*
  ñúe jíibina fɨnódɨmɨe   *jm* jm
  afeno méíñote.   *jm* jm
Nɨga ñuera úai   10
  buináimamo ite daɨnano.   *jm* jm
Meita uafue
  buináimamo ñuefue ite, manaɨfue ite, naɨméredɨfue ite,   *jm*
  komuiya jagɨyɨ ite,   *jm* jm
  kaɨ kaziya jagɨyɨ ite, kaɨ   15
  jafírikaiya jagɨyɨ ite.   *jm* jm

Daɨnánona
  fueñe jitókomena yezika   *jm* jm
  jíibie dute   *jm* jm
  dɨona fɨnode,   *jm* jm   20
  ie
  kakáreikano fɨnode,   *jm* jm
  daama ie moo dɨga úrite.   *jm* jm
Ie jira, buinaima komékɨmo itɨfuena onóakadɨkue, daɨde,   *jm*
  buinaima komékɨmo ite kaɨ komuiya jɨɨrana onóakadɨkue.   *jm* 25
Ie jira
  moo dɨnena daɨde,   *jm*
  mei o rátiadɨ   *jm*
  o káaniadɨ   *jm* jm
  nia mei kákaitɨo.   *jm* jm   30

Text 9
How We Were Formed
By the Word of Tobacco and Coca

Well then, although
  in this way
  there are good teachings,
  these teachings are in the heart of the *buinaima*.[1]
And so, how are we going to remove them from his heart?   5
Well then, because it is said that the *buinaima* possesses this wisdom
  he who prepares good tobacco,
  he who prepares coca
  studies this point.
How many good words   10
  are there in the *buinaima?* he thus asks.
And, in truth,
  the *buinaima* has good teachings, cool teachings, sweet teachings,
  he has the breath of life,
  he has the breath of our awakening,   15
  he has the breath of tranquility.

So, it is said that
  when a young man, for the first time,
  mambes coca,
  and prepares tobacco,   20
  he
  prepares it watchfully
  and he talks, alone, to his father.
Well then, "I want to learn all that there is in the heart of the *buinaima*," he says,
  "I want to learn the spells of life that there are in the heart of the *buinaima*." 25
Well then,
  the father tells him,
  "If you sit down,
  if you stay watchful,
  then you will feel it."   30

Ñúe íitɨoza, daɨde,   *jm*
  nia mei ónoitɨo, daɨde.   *jm* jm
Ie jira
  uafue, daɨde.   *jm* jm
Dɨona komúitari, daɨde,   *jm*   35
  jíibina komúitari, daɨde,   *jm*
  daama, daɨde,   *jm* jm
  nɨɨa uaina o yotɨkue, daɨde.   *jm*

Ie jira
  fueñe jíibie dutɨmɨe   40
  ja ua afeno fɨnote,   *jm* jɨɨ
  afénona onóakade.   *jm*
Ie jira dɨona daɨde, jíibina daɨde, ja
  jíibina komúitajano, dɨona komúitajano
  ja jenode.   *jm*   45
Jenode, afedo
  ja jɨfaide,   *jm* jm
  mei buináimamo ite daɨna jira.   *jm* jm
Ie jira ua afedo ua dukano ua bite,   *jm* jɨɨ
  ua dɨónado jɨfáikano bite.   *jm* jm   50

Ua bite, bite, bite, ua
  afénori ja ua nabedɨ jíibina komuide,   *jm*
  nabedɨ farékatofe komuide,   *jm*
  nabedɨ mazákarɨ komuide.   *jm*
Ie mei ja afedo   55
  ie úiñoye,   *jm* jm
  fueñe komuide jíibina abɨri ja
    jɨɨra fakade,   *jm*
  fueñe komuide dɨona abɨri ja
    jɨɨra fakade,   *jm* jɨɨ   60
  fueñe komuide farékatofe abɨri jɨaɨ
    jɨɨra fakade,   *jm* jɨɨ
  mazákarɨ abɨri
    jɨɨra fakade.   *jm* jm jm
Ie jenuizaɨ baiyena,   *jm* jm   65

"If you live well," he says,
   "you will learn," he says.
Well then,
   "It is true," the young man says.
"You have to grow tobacco," the father says,   35
   "you have to grow coca," he says,
   "by yourself," he says,
   "I am telling you the true word," he says.

Well then,
   the one who *mambes* coca for the first time   40
   truly believes in that,
   because he wants to learn about that.
Well then, he works the tobacco, he works the coca;
   and once he has his own plants of tobacco and coca,
   now he searches.   45
He searches, and with that[2]
   he gets drunk,
   because it is said that these teachings are in the heart of the *buinaima.*
Well then, with that, he keeps *mambeing,*
   he keeps getting drunk with tobacco.   50

He keeps and keeps and keeps on doing that, and
   there comes a point when the genuine plant of coca is born,
   the genuine plant of sweet manioc is born,
   the genuine plant of peanut is born.[3]
And then, with that Word,   55
   he will care for them.
   At the side of the first plant of coca that grows, now,
      he tries out the spells,
   at the side of the first plant of tobacco that grows, now,
      he tries out the spells,   60
   at the side of the first plant of sweet manioc that grows,
      he also tries out the spells,
   at the side of the plant of peanut,
      he tries out the spells.
To discover their diseases,   65

dɨona jenuizaɨ baiyena, *jm*
jíibina jenuizaɨ baiyena,   *jm* jm
farékatofe jenuizaɨ baiyena,   *jm* jm
mazákarɨ jenuizaɨ baiyena,   *jm* jm
afena kɨóiyena.   *jm* jm jm   70
Ie jira
ua jenókano uite,   *jm*
ja jíibina káadote, dɨona káadote, ja
farékatofe káadote,   *jm* jɨɨ
mazákarɨ káadote,   *jm* jɨɨ jɨɨ   75
onóakade   *jm* jm
afénona.   *jm* jm
Iedo
ja ua afénona onode,   *jm* jm
ja ua dɨona jɨɨrana kakade,   *jm*   80
jíibina jɨɨrana kakade,   *jm* jɨɨ
farékatofe jɨɨrana kakade,   *jm*
mazákarɨ jɨɨrana kakade.   *jm* jɨɨ

Ie izoi eróikano
itɨno jae   85
mooma mei kuemo yote.   *jm* jm
Ie meita jenókano uitɨkue ua
afeno ua káadokano uitɨkue,   *jm* jɨɨ jm
jizákuru abɨri.   *jm* jm jm
Mei jenoka úai   90
be daɨi ja ua yoyena,   *jm* jm jm
ñuéfuena itɨno-   *jm*
   -na ite,   *jm* jm jm
kome úrue ua ɨrákotaiyana onóiyena,   *jm* jɨɨ
kome úrue jenúitaifiyana onóiyena,   *jm* jm jm   95
kome úrue ua zɨékotaiyana onóiyena,   *jm* jm
kome úrue tɨzítaiyana onóiyena.   *jm* jm jm
Akɨ dɨno jenode,   *jm* jm
ic jira ñúe onóiyena.   *jm* jm jm

                                                              [ii]
Idɨ úai bie izóikano ja yúa jira,   100

                          248

to discover the diseases in tobacco,
to discover the diseases in coca,
to discover the diseases in sweet manioc,
to discover the diseases in peanut,
to see that.   70
Well then,
he keeps on searching,
he watches over the coca plant, watches over the tobacco plant,
watches over the plant of sweet manioc,
watches over the plant of peanut;   75
he wants to learn
about that.
That is why
now truly, he learns about that,
now truly, he hears the spells of tobacco,   80
he hears the spells of coca,
he hears the spells of sweet manioc,
he hears the spells of peanut.

In a similar manner,
formerly,   85
my father told me these things.
And so, I have kept searching, truly,
I have kept watchful
at the side of the children.
The word I have sought out   90
is to be told as it is;
it is
a good knowledge,
to learn about the diseases of one's child,
to learn about the pollution in one's child,   95
to learn about the evils that happen to one's child,
to learn about the paralysis of one's child.
One searches these points,
to learn well.

                                                                        [ii]
Because this true word is as I am relating it,   100

dɨnómonanɨbaɨyoga
daɨnana eroide.   *jm* jm jɨɨ
Ñénidɨnomona arɨ
   ua ja kakana úai
   fia be daɨi yoga.   *jm* jɨɨ jɨɨ   105
Iena mei onóñedɨmɨe taɨno daɨde,   *jm* jm
   daɨna abɨna úa raana ite mei uaina ite,   *jm* jɨɨ
   jagɨyɨna ite,   *jm* jɨɨ jɨɨ
   ua raana itɨno.   *jm* jm jm
Iena ímɨe baitade,   110
   ímɨe ziiño   *jm*
   daɨnana eroide,   *jm*
   zíiñoñede,   *jm*
   baitáñede;   *jm* jm
   fia jíibina ie fɨmaiya úai,   *jm*   115
   dɨona ie fɨmaiya úai.   *jm* jɨɨ jɨɨ
Ie izóikana itɨno mei bie yoina,   *jm* jɨɨ
   jɨaɨma éikome ua komekɨ ífueñede,   *jm* jɨɨ
   jɨaɨma éikome mei batɨ danɨ imakɨ
   jitókome onoiga.   *jm* jɨɨ   120

Ie izoide bie jae kue jíibie kue fɨnua yezika
   kue fɨnua úai,
   kue kakana úai mei yotɨkue.   *jm*
Ie izoi fui
   úrue komúiadɨ oni yoyena.   *jm* jm   125
Ie jira ja kue úrue komuide,   *jm* jm
   ja jitókome naidaide, ja éikomena ite.   *jm*
Ie jira aféɨe
   úrue anamo ja komuide.   *jm* jm
Iena kɨóiyano   *jm*   130
   ja, uzu, ja kuena daɨdɨno ite.   *jm* jɨɨ jɨɨ

Ie jira
   ja birui yoyena   *jm*
   afe úai,   *jm*
   ja kakana úai   *jm* jm   135

it might seem that it is
something I just invented.
Out of the impossible,
  truly now, I obtained this word,
  and today I am relating it this way.   105
And he who does not know says it is not true;
  he might say so, but this word has power, has substance,
  has breath—
  these are Things of power.
And it might seem   110
  that one is a sorcerer,
  that one has supernatural abilities;
  but this is not sorcery,
  these are not supernatural abilities,
  it is just the word of the discipline of coca,   115
  the word of the discipline of tobacco.
This is the kind of thing I am relating,
  these are not another elder's ideas;
  what belongs to other elders is known only
  to their apprentices.   120

Likewise, this is the word I followed when I learnt
  to prepare coca,
  the word I heard is what I tell you now.
So that later,
  when your children are born, you can tell them.   125
Well then, my children were already born,
  they already grew up, they are becoming old.
Well then, to them
  already new children were born.
I have seen them,   130
  and now, there is somebody who calls me grandfather.

Well then,
  that word today
  is to be told;
  what today is heard   135

jae jíibie dúa uaina ite.   *jm jɨɨ jɨɨ*
Uafue uzuma yote, fui imakɨ dáɨiyena;   *jm jm jm*
  kue uzúmana kɨódɨkue,   *jm jm*
  ie yezika uzuma mei akɨ daɨi úriya,   *jm jɨɨ*
dáɨiyena.   *jm jm jm*   140

Baɨ ba éinamakɨ mei yogafue ite,   *jm jm*
  afena kue onóñedɨkue.   *jm jm jm*
Meita akɨ dɨno akie izóikano ite úai
  fia mei bie jɨfánua izoi yoga.   *jm jm jm*
Daama kome ua afeno ua ba fɨnotɨmɨe komékɨmo mei ite,   *jm jɨɨ*   145
  fɨnoñedɨmɨe komékɨmo mei iñede,   *jm*
  fia uaina ite.   *jm jɨɨ jɨɨ*
Ie izoi eróikano mei ite jenókanona itɨno,   *jm jɨɨ*
  neemei birui fia jíibie dutɨzamo ite, iñede.   *jm jɨɨ jɨɨ*

Ie izoi mei   150
  ua ba ráfuedo bitɨmɨe úriya uáiita ñeiri,
  mei daaje íadɨ bie mei ua
  daama ba jíibie úrue eróikano ua fɨnódɨmɨe mei akɨ daɨi úrite.
                                                               jm jɨɨ
Meita daaje izoide ua dáɨinide.   *jm jm jm*
Ie mei kue yɨɨnua úai fia kue yɨɨnua jagɨyɨna ite,   *jm jm jm*   155
  ie ua ba nɨnona eroide.   *jm jm jm*

                                                               [iii]
Ie izóikano ba
  eiño dɨbene,   *jm jɨɨ*
  farékatofe ie komúitaja úai mei manáɨdɨno iya,   *jm*
    ie fɨnoka farékatofe úai naɨmere iya,   *jm jɨɨ*   160
  mazákarɨ úai manaɨ iya,   *jm jɨɨ*
  juzítofe úai manaɨ iya,   *jm jm jm*
  tubujɨ úai manaɨ iya,   *jm jm*
  jakáizairai úai manaɨ iya,   *jm jm jm*
  jifirai úai manaɨ iya,   *jm jɨɨ*   165
  ɾɨɨrcdc ia akɨ dáɨitade komekɨ íadɨ fɨnókaza
  mei ua naɨmérede.   *jm jɨɨ*
Ie eiño ja ua dɨnori mei ja ua

is the word with which I have *mambed* coca.
"What grandfather told is true," so they will later say;
  "I saw my grandfather,
  and he used to speak this way,"
  so they will say.   140

The elders of other places tell other things,
  but, about that, I do not know.
And so, these things are like that,
  and it might seem that when I tell it, I am playing a game.
These things are only in the heart of he who believes and obeys,   145
  they are not in the heart of the disbeliever—
  they are, but only in words.
Thus are the things I have sought out.
  Does the one who only *mambe* coca have them?[4] He does not.

Thus,   150
  this is not the conversation which comes from the tradition of
                                               dancing rituals,
  although they belong together. Only
  he who prepares his coca thinking of his children speaks this way.
And so, one cannot say it is the same thing.
This is simply the word I received, the breath I received,   155
  even if it seems like another thing.

                                                                     [iii]
In a similar manner
  is the part of the Mother—
  the word for making the sweet manioc grow is calm,
    the word for preparing the sweet manioc is sweet,   160
  the word of peanut is calm,
  the word of bitter manioc is calm,
  the word of *daledale* is calm,
  the word of yam is calm,
  the word of chili pepper is calm,   165
  she works them with this heart, and although that word is difficult
  it becomes sweet.
And the Mother, from then on,

ua ja jiza zairítate,   *jm*
ja jitáigona naidaide.   *jm* jii   170
Ie kióiyanona ja
nabéfuena ja aiyo oni ua fúunote,   *jm* jii
aiyo oni ua zaiónote.   *jm* jii jii
Ie izoi eróikano eiño dibene ite.   *jm* jm jm

Meita dinori jiira fakáiadi,   175
moo, daide,   *jm*
oni eiño, daide,   *jm* jii
ari kai komúitakano atide,   *jm* jii
ari kai jagiyi móonaitakano atide.   *jm* jii
Ie izóikano ite   180
moo ibe uabe, eiño ibe uabe.   *jm*

COMMENTARY ON TEXT 9:
"HOW WE WERE FORMED BY THE WORD OF TOBACCO AND COCA"

Kinerai tells us that when a task ends, the *buinaima* comes. He comes with the rains at the end of the year, when the work of the garden has finished and the clearing of next year's garden has still not been done. The spirit of the *buinaima* comes to complete the tasks of the year, and with him the rain comes, because the *buinaima* is the rain man. At that time of the year, people spend more time at home, weaving baskets and making tools, and in the site of the coca ritual the men speak as Kinerai does in this text.

I place this speech, which was recorded at the end of a year of investigation, at the end of the book in order to close this collection of texts. After the Mother and the Father have finished their work (texts 7 and 8) the spirit speaks to complete and cool down all that has been said. Here Kinerai recapitulates his life since the time when he began to *mambe* coca (section i). This is a confirmation of the Word of tobacco and coca. The words collected in these texts, Kinerai states, are not momentary inventions, neither are they stories he heard from other people. These words were formed by the work of tobacco and

raises her daughter,
    she becomes a big girl.   170
Seeing that,
    resolutely the mother strongly blows,
    she strongly tempers.
Such is the work of the Mother.

And so, from then on, when one makes a spell,   175
    one says "Father,"
    and also says "Mother,
    you have been helping us to grow,
    you have been increasing our breath of life."
So it is   180
    the true Leaf of the Father, the true Leaf of the Mother.

---

coca, and through the study of the development of "creatures": tobacco, coca, sweet manioc, peanut—boys and girls. He speaks like that because he obeys the restrictions, sits to meditate, *mambes,* gets drunk, searches in the Bottom of the World, fetches, makes dawn. Because it is true, one can see it in the gardens, and in the children that grow up—"and now, there is somebody who calls me grandfather" (line 131).

In section ii he defends his work and reasserts his authority (lines 103-109):

Out of the impossible,
    truly now, I obtained this word,
    and today I am relating it this way.
And he who does not know says it is not true;
    he might say so, but this word has power, has substance,
    has breath—
    these are Things of power.

"Out of the impossible"—literally, "from where it is forbidden"—means that it is a knowledge obtained by means of drunkenness *(jɨfaiya);* it allows him to travel to the Bottom of the World *(biko jiyákimo).* There, all things (plants, creatures) exist only as breath *(jagɨyɨ).* He brings that breath and instills it into the Mother; the Mother becomes ill *(zegore ite)* with that breath. To heal her, one has to work and turn that breath into true Things *(úa rafue).* When these things become real, one "sees" them *(kɨoide).* These are Things of power *(raana itɨno).*

Dance ritual

As the *buinaima*'s heart appears after a year of work, so he manifests himself at the end of a day of work, during the night, when, after preparing his coca, a man sits to meditate and talk. His body cools down, and with that breath he cools down everything. Then, it is said that he is seated as a *buinaima*—his heart is cool and peaceful (lines 13-16):

> And, in truth,
>> the *buinaima* has good teachings, cool teachings, sweet teachings,
>> he has the breath of life,
>> he has the breath of our awakening,
>> he has the breath of tranquility.

At that moment, Kɨnerai says, everything cools down: in the garden, the plant of coca, the plant of tobacco, the plant of sweet manioc are cool and fresh—their breath is *riérue*, "like dew," and *jírue* "like moist clay." Likewise, in the house everything cools down: the stove, the cassava bread, all the tools; and likewise, he says, the woman sleeps peacefully as a plant of sweet manioc, and the children sleep as plants of coca and plants of peanut.

This is the conversation of tobacco and coca of a family man. A master of dance rituals has this same *buinaima* conversation, but it is only uttered during the times when he prepares and performs the rituals, and can only be expressed in elaborate mythological terms. That is why Kɨnerai says (lines 150-154):

> Thus,
>> this is not the conversation which comes from the tradition of dancing
> rituals,
>> although they belong together. Only
>> he who prepares his coca thinking of his children speaks this way.

In section iii he invokes the work of the Mother. This same spirit of the *buinaima* cools down all the works of the Mother, her word of sweet manioc, peanut, bitter manioc—everything becomes sweet and calm.

Finally, he concludes with a spell (lines 175-179):

> And so, from then on, when one makes a spell,
>> one says "Father,"
>> and also says "Mother,
>> you have been helping us to grow,
>> you have been increasing our breath of life."

APPENDICES

CULTIVATED PLANT SPECIES

ABBREVIATIONS: aff.: affinity to - sp.: species - spp.: species (pl.) - var.:variety - indet.: indeterminate

English Name*	Scientific Name	Uitoto Names
MAIN PLANTS		
Tobacco	Solanaceae *Nicotiana tabacum*	*díue* (generic); *diona* (plant); *diobe* (leaf); *dioji* (seed); *dióyeki* (flower); *diore* (plantation)
Coca	Erythroxylaceae *Erythroxylum coca* var. *ipadu*	*júibie* (generic); *júibina* (plant); *júibibe* (leave); *júibidozi* (stem); *júibikoǵo* (heap of leaves); *júibire* (plantation)
Sweet Manioc[†]	Euphorbiaceae *Manihot esculenta*	*fareka* (generic); *farékatofe* (stem); *farékaji* (tuber); *farékare* (plantation)
Bitter Manioc[†]	(idem)	*júe* (generic); *juzítofe* (stem); *juji* (tuber); *júzie* (plantation)
Edible Manioc[†]	(idem)	*maika* (generic); *máikatofe* (stem); *máikaji* (tuber)
Pineapple	Bromeliaceae *Ananas comosus*	*rozídoro* (plant); *roziyi* (fruit); *rozire* (plantation)
Peanut	Leguminoseae *Arachis hypogeae*	*mazaka* (generic); *mazákari* (plant); *mazákaji* (seed); *mazákare* (plantation)
Chili pepper	Solanaceae *Capsicum chinense; Capsicum frutescens*	*jifirai* (plant); *jifiji* (fruit); *jífiruǵo* (seed)
OTHER TUBERS		
Arrowroot	Marantaceae *Maranta ruiziiana*	*chikipira* (plant)
Canna lily	Cannaceae *Canna* aff. *edulis*	*bediǵo* (corm); *bediji* (fruit); *bedícheri* (seedling)
Cocoyam	Araceae *Xanthosoma* sp.	*duna* (generic); *dunayi* (plant); *dunaji* (tuber)

260

English Name*	Scientific Name	Uitoto Names
Daledale	Marantaceae *Calathea* sp.	*tuburɨ* (plant); *tubujɨ* (corm)
Sweet potato	Convolvulaceae *Ipomoea batatas*	*refijɨ* (tuber); *refio* (stem)
Taro	Araceae *Colocasia* aff. *esculenta*	*enokakiyɨ* (plant); *enókabe* (leaf); *enókajɨ* (tuber)
Taro, white people's	Araceae *Colocasia* sp.1	*duna rɨaɨ ie* (generic)
White taro	Araceae *Colocasia* sp.2	*uragoɨ* (plant); *urajɨ* (tuber)
Yam	Dioscoreaceae *Dioscorea trifida*	*jakáizairai* (plant); *jakáio* (stem); *jakáijɨ* (tuber); *jakáie* (plantation)
Yam bean	Leguminosae *Pachyrhizus tuberosus*	*goizeño* (fruit); *goizedo* (seed)

FRUIT TREES

Anon	Annonaceae *Rollinia mucosa*	*toguena* (tree); *toguedo* (seed); *togueyɨ* (fruit)
Avocado	Lauraceae *Persea americana*	*nomena* (tree); *nomedo* (fruit)
Breadfruit tree	Moraceae *Batocarpus amazonicus*	*uibirai* (tree); *uibijɨ* (seed); *uibiyɨ* (fruit)
Cacao	Sterculiaceae *Theobroma bicolor*	*mɨzena* (tree); *mɨzeyɨ* (fruit); *mɨzedo* (seed)
Forest grape	Cecropiaceae *Pourouma cecropiifolia*	*jɨrikue* (generic); *jɨrikona* (tree); *jɨrikojɨ* (fruit); *jɨrikodo* (seed); *jɨrikore* (plantation)
Inga	Leguminosae Mimosoideae *Inga edulis; Inga macrocarpa*	*jizáiñue* (generic); *jizairai* (tree); *jizaiño* (fruit); *jizaido* (seed)
Peach palm	Palmae *Bactris gasipaes*	jimena *(palm);* jimekɨ *(fruit);* jimedo *(seed)*
Sapote	Sapotaceae *Pouteria caimito*	*jɨfikue* (generic); *jɨfikona* (tree); *jɨfikoyɨ* (fruit); *jɨfikodo* (seed)
Umari, black *(goido)*	Icacinaceae *Poraqueiba sericea*	*goirai* (tree); *goido* (fruit)
Umari, black *(obedo)*	(idem)	*oberai* (tree); *obedo* (fruit)

261

English Name*	Scientific Name	Uitoto Names
Umari, green	(idem)	*nekana* (tree); *nekazɨ* (fruit); *nekároki* (seedling)
Umari, yellow	(idem)	*nemona* (tree); *nemozɨ* (fruit)

GRASSES

Maize	Gramineae *Zea mays*	*beya* (generic); *beyado* (cob); *beyajɨ* (kernel)
Sugar cane	Gramineae *Saccharum* sp.	*konónue* (generic)

MEDICINAL PLANTS

Basil	Labiatae *Ocimum* sp.	*jaibikɨ* (plant)
[medicinal plant]	Compositae	*dirɨmao* (stems); *dirɨmabe* (leaf)
[medicinal plant]	(indet.)	*naɨmeki*
[medicinal plant]	(indet.)	*nozekue*
[medicinal plant]	(indet.)	*katubai*
[medicinal plant]	(indet.)	*yinakai*
[plant to conjure the eyes]	Apocynaceae *Bonafousia tetrastachya*	*jifɨkona* (plant)

* English names of species are mostly from Joe Salick's review of the literature on crops grown by various Amazonian groups (Salick 1989, appendix). Names in italics are from Spanish.

† "Manioc" stands for the plant of *Manihot,* and "cassava" for the bread obtained from its tubers (following the usage of Christine Hugh-Jones 1979). Manioc and Cassava often appear as synonyms in the literature. "Sweet" manioc is a variety of the "bitter" (poisonous) manioc, which is very rich in juice; it is only used for the preparation of a ritual drink called *juiñoi*.

APPENDIX 2
OTHER PLANT SPECIES

ABBREVIATIONS: sp.: species - spp.: species (pl.)

English Name*	Scientific Name	Uitoto Names
Bacaba	Palmae *Oenocarpus bacaba*	*gurikaɨ* (palm); *gurɨofe* (fiber)
Brazil nut	Lecythidaceae *Bertholettia excelsa*	*ifákɨe* (generic); *ifákɨna* (tree); *ifákɨdo* (nut)
Cecropia tree	Cecropiaceae *Cecropia sciadophylla*	*kɨraikaɨ* (generic); *uákɨraikaɨ* (proper); *ɨmuizaɨ* (ashes)
Cumare palm	Palmae *Astrocaryum aculeatum* (= *A. chambira*)	*ñekɨna* (palm); *ñekɨkɨ* (fruit); *ñekɨdo* (thorn); *ñekɨro* (fiber)
Guarumo	Marantaceae *Ischnosiphon aruma*	*ñotakaɨ* (stem); *ñotáofe* (fiber)
Juansoco	Apocynaceae *Couma macrocarpa*	*ikikaɨ* (tree); *ikikɨ* (fruit)
Miriti palm	Palmae *Mauritia flexuosa*	*kinena* (palm); *kinekɨ* (fruit)
Yaripa palm	Palmae *Dictyocaryum ptariense*	*jikɨfena* (palm)
[Sources of tobacco mixture:]	Malpigiaceae Rapateaceae *Rapatea* sp.	*marákɨo* (vine) *eraguaɨ*
[Sources of vegetable salt:]	Araceae *Spathiphyllum cannaefolium*	*zúuie*
	Lecythidaceae *Eschweilera itayensis*	*jafena* (tree)
	Lecythidaceae *Gustavia poeppigiana*	*jerogɨ* (tree)
	Palmae *Astrocaryum gynacanthum*	*ruirigɨ* (palm); *ruiriyɨ* (palm heart)
	Palmae *Bactris hirta*	*jodajimena* (palm)
	Palmae *Bactris riparia*	*jimáikɨe*
	Palmae *Desmoncus* sp.	*turao*
	Palmae *Maximiliana maripa*	*jarɨna* (palm); *jarɨyɨ* (palm heart); *jarɨgoraɨ* (bark)
	Sterculiaceae *Theobroma subincanum*	*mɨñɨekona* (tree)
	(indet.)	*chapena* (tree)

*Names in italics are from Spanish.

263

APPENDIX 3
ANIMAL SPECIES

ABBREVIATION: spp.: species (pl.)

English Name*	Scientific Name	Uitoto Names
INVERTEBRATES		
Grubs	Order Coleoptera: *Rhina palmarum; Calandra palmarum*	*ziaiki*
Termites	Order Isoptera	*karákigo* (one); *karaiai* (many)
REPTILES		
Speckled cayman	Alligatoridae *Caiman sclerops* (= *C. crocodylus*)	*zeema*
BIRDS		
Great tinamou	Tinamidae *Tinamus major*	*ofoma* (generic); *uáfoma* (true)
Hawk	Accipitridae *Accipiter bicolor*	*nuiki*
MAMMALS		
Black jaguar	Felidae *Felis yagouaroundi*	*jiko* (generic); *zurúyari*
Coati; Coatimundis	Procyonidae *Nasua nasua*	*nimaido*
Collared peccary	Tayassuidae *Tayassu tajacu*	*mero*
[Edible mouse]	Echimiydae *Proechimys* spp.	*míñie*
Fresh water dolphin	Platanistidae *Inia geoffrensis*	*amana; buinaima*
Giant anteater	Myrmecophagidae *Myrmecophaga tridactyla*	*ereño*
Giant armadillo	Dasypodidae *Priodontes maximus*	*bainaago*
Jaguar	Felidae *Panthera onca*	*jiko* (generic); *janáyari*

264

English Name*	Scientific Name	Uitoto Names
Kinkajou	Procyonidae *Potos flavus; Bassaricyon gabbii*	*kuita*
Ocelot *(F. pardalis)*; Margay *(F. wiedii)*	Felidae *Felis wiedii; Felis pardalis*	*jɨko* (generic); *jirako* (true); *nonódoko; ekúirodozi*
Paca	Agoutidae *Agouti paca*	*ɨme*
Prehensile-tailed porcupine	Erethizontidae *Coendu prehensilis*	*juku*
Small agouti	Dasyproctidae *Myoprocta acouchy*	*mɨgui*
Small armadillo; Spurred armadillo *(D. kappleri)*	Dasypodidae *Dasypus novemcinctus; Dasypus kappleri*	*uánɨgo; ñenɨgo; nákonɨgo; kovero*
Tamandua	Myrmecophagidae *Tamandua tetradactyla*	*doboyi*
Tapir	Tapiridae *Tapirus terrestris*	*zuruma*
Three-toed sloth	Bradypodidae *Bradypus variegatus*	*yaiño*
Titi monkey	Cebidae *Callicebus torquatus*	*aikɨ*
White-lipped peccary	Tayassuidae *Tayassu pecari*	*eimoɨ*
Woolly monkey	Cebidae *Lagothrix lagothricha*	*jemɨ*

*English names of species are mostly from John C. Kricher, *A Neotropical Companion* (1989).

NOTES

INTRODUCTION

1. The Colombian government has recently recognized 18,724,540 hectares (that is, 46,380,685 acres, over half of the Colombian Amazon) as legally belonging to the indigenous races who have traditionally lived there, under a legal figure called "preserves" *(Resguardos)* (Roldán Ortega 1993). Such preserves are different from "reservations" in the U.S. sense in that they grant legal ownership of the land to the natives, whereas on reservations the government grants the use of the land to inhabitants but retains property rights.

2. Some researchers have proposed utilizing the term "Murui-Muinane" to describe the language and ethnic group which is commonly known in anthropological literature as "Huitoto" or "Witoto." The term "huitoto," which is of Carib origin, is a pejorative one which the Carijona groups employed to designate their tribal enemies and it was adopted by rubber-traders and missionaries to designate these tribes; subsequently the term came to be widely employed in scientific and official documents. I agree with those researchers that the term should be rejected, but this same indigenous group, the "Huitotos," has decided to conserve the title, modifying its spelling to "Uitoto," which is consistent with the alphabet which has been adopted to write down that language. For this reason I use the term in this book with its new spelling.

The Uitoto Indians live in the Colombo-Peruvian Amazon, mainly along the Caquetá, Igaraparaná, Caraparaná, Putumayo, Amazonas and Ampiyacu rivers. Their total population today, in both countries, is approximately 8,000. Their language belongs to the Uitoto linguistic family, which also includes the Okaina and Nonuya languages. This small family of languages does not seem to be related to any other linguistic family in the Amazon basin. Main published sources on the ethnography of this group are: Koch-Grünberg (1906), Whiffen (1915), Preuss (1921-1923, 1994), Steward (1948), Gasché (1975, 1977), and Pineda (1987). On the history of rubber exploitation in the Putumayo region under the notorious Casa Arana, which caused the death and forced resettlement of many Indians during the first half of this century, see: Casement (1911), Hardenburg (1912), Taussig (1987), and Domínguez and Gómez (1994).

3. To *mambe* means to ingest coca by putting *"mambe"* inside the cheeks, where it is slowly absorbed through the mouth and digestive tissues. *Mambe:* powder obtained by toasting, pounding and straining coca leaves, with the addition of ashes of leaves from the cecropia tree. As this action does not correspond to "to eat coca" or "to chew coca," this new verb, borrowed from Spanish, is introduced: *mambe, mambed, mambeing.*

4. The vegetable salt is a precipitate obtained by filtering water through the ashes of several plants, mainly palms (see "Source of vegetable salt" in appendix 2). See also note 2 to text 6A for an explanation of the method of preparing vegetable salt.

5. Ernesto Cardenal, *Antología de poesía primitiva* (1979, 16) (my English translation).

6. This form of poetic presentation of indigenous texts has been practiced for the last two decades by several American researchers who belong to what has been called the school of ethnopoetics. The following works have been an important source of inspiration and guidance for my work: Dell Hymes, *"In Vain I Tried To Tell You": Essays in Native American Ethnopoetics* (1981); Dennis Tedlock, *The Spoken Word and the Work of Interpretation* (1983); Joel Sherzer, *Verbal Art in San Blas* (1990); and Brian Swann, ed., *On the Translation of Native American Literatures* (1992).

7. Argemiro Candre, another son of Kɨneraɨ, was the conversation partner in texts 2A and 2B; I myself was the partner of texts 3A and 8A; in all other texts, the conversation partner was Kɨneraɨ's son Blas, with the exception of text 1, which had no partner.

8. The following is the chronological order of the texts (all dates are from 1992): April 2 (text 6A), April 8 (text 2A), April 9 (text 2B), April 12 (text 6B), April 17 (texts 2 and 3), April 20 (text 4), April 22 (texts 5, 6, 7, and 8), July 2 (text 3A), July 6 (text 1), August 27 (text 8A), September 17 (text 3B), and September 27 (text 9).

9. Words which were barely audible are transcribed between parentheses.

10. In 1994 there appeared an excellent translation of Preuss' book into Spanish, by Eudocio Becerra (Bigɨdɨma) and Gabriele Petersen de Piñeros (Preuss 1994). Becerra, a Uitoto Indian who speaks the same dialect of Preuss' informants, and Petersen de Piñeros, a German-born linguist who lives in Colombia, not only translated Preuss' German text into Spanish but undertook a full review of the Uitoto text and of Preuss' German translation from Uitoto. Becerra and Petersen de Piñeros, nevertheless, did not translate Preuss' dictionary, from which most of my references are taken: "The original dictionary (Uitoto-German) was not consulted for the present work due to some deficiencies in it (lack of vocables, confusion among similar but not identical terms, inclusion of terms which do not appear in the texts)" (Becerra and Petersen de Piñeros, in Preuss 1994, 2:791). On the other hand, they elaborated a new dictionary from an alphabetical list of all the terms contained in the texts, revised and transcribed by them.

COMMENTARY ON TEXT 1

1. The common term for "word" is *úai,* which I translate as "word" without capitals. See the alternation of the two uses in lines-69-71.

2. The common term for "thing, object" is *raa,* which I translate as "thing" without capitals.

3. This refers to the practice, in the dance rituals, of exchanging cultivated food, produced by the ritual master and his relatives, for wild game and songs brought by the invited groups.

TEXT 2A

1. In this text Kɨneraɨ uses some words in the *búe* dialect. The corresponding words in the *minika* dialect are the following:

BÚE DIALECT	*MƗNƗKA* DIALECT	ENGLISH
keiño	*eiño*	mother
jeraimo	*eromo*	in the womb
jafaikɨ	*jagɨyɨ*	breath
ie fakaize	*ie yezika*	in that moment
naie	*afe*	that
naino	*afeno*	that issue
fɨraiñote	*jɨɨde*	cure

COMMENTARY ON TEXTS 2 AND 2A

1. Also: "breath of termite *karánui"* means tamandua; "breath of dry wood" means prehensile-tailed porcupine; "breath of the fungus *yamórue"* means ocelot; "breath of the grass *naimeki"* means giant anteater; "breath of hunger" means edible mouse; "breath of brazil nut" means jaguar; "breath of *anon"* means kinkajou. Dietary habits explain some of these relations, as is the case of the white-lipped peccary which eats *cumare* fruits, the woolly monkey which eats *juansoco* fruits, the tamandua which eats termites, and the prehensile-tailed porcupine which eats dry wood. Morphological analogy explains others: the fruit of the green *umari* is greasy, like tapir's meat; the peel of the fruit of black *umari* is dark, like the collared peccary, and its pulp is greasy, like the peccary's meat; the fruit of the brazil nut tree resembles the head of a jaguar; the pulp of *anon* is like the fat of kinkajou. The edible mouse is called "breath of hunger" because "it is very hungry" (eats a lot).

The appendices contain the biological identification of all plants and animals mentioned.

TEXT 2B

1. See commentary on texts 3 and 3A for a description of the armadillo basket and an explanation of its symbolism.

2. The cassava cake is thicker and softer than the cassava bread. The cassava bread is made with dry manioc meal baked on the griddle; the cassava cake is made with the same cassava meal plus water and baked on the griddle wrapped in heliconia leaves.

COMMENTARY ON TEXT 2B

1. The story of Amenakudu and Amenakuriño.

2. See the myth of "Monaiya Jurama" in Konɨraga, Toɨrabuinaima ie Juzigɨtofe (1988, 9-10).

3. The biologist Olga L. Montenegro researched the different plant-animal relations that appear in the notes and carried out a first version of the translation into Spanish of this text, which I used as a reference for the present version.

4. This dream and the next one are not proper dreams of abundance but bad dreams. It seems that Kɨneraɨ brought in these two dreams inadvertently, but then he did not continue along that line.

TEXT 3

1. The Uitoto word *mirɨgo* refers specifically to the sister of a man. See also the commentary on the text.

2. The Uitoto word *ɨio* refers specifically to the brother of a woman. See also the commentary on the text.

3. *ɨrɨgɨ:* fish trap woven with vines in the shape of a round basket; it has a wide mouth and a narrow neck.

4. *Zeda:* fish trap made with long stripes from the heart of palm leaves tied with vines, in the form of a long basket, narrow at the bottom and wider in the mouth.

5. The boy weaves a small basket and brings bark strips and heliconia leaves from the forest; the girl, in the house, ties the bark strips to the basket and lines it with the leaves—that is the girl's work.

TEXT 3A

1. Cecropia trees grow rapidly soon after a garden is abandoned.

2. See description of the *ibigaɨ* basket in the commentary on text 3.

3. *Kovero:* name of another species of armadillo (indet.)

4. *Ñenɨgaɨ* means "basket of small armadillo." Both *ñenɨgaɨ* and *ibigaɨ* are narrow-weave baskets; the characteristic of the armadillo basket is that the holes are hexagonal, whereas the other's holes are pentagonal.

Hexagonal holes

5. *Jebogaɨ* is an open-weave basket; see its description in the commentary on text 3.

6. Lining it with heliconia leaves.

7. The Bottom of This World: the east.

8. There are male and female thunders. A male thunder happens in a single burst or explosion: *"huuuu zeeche!"*, whereas the female thunder is rolling and prolonged: *"tiii-ri-ri-ri-ri-ri."* If the latter happens in an eastern direction, this is the giant armadillo's thunder—she is making that big, heavy earthenware pot slowly turn around.

Pentagonal holes

COMMENTARY ON TEXTS 3 AND 3A

1. The suffix *-ra* in *yera* stands for "thing, substance." Thus, *yera* could also be interpreted as "substance of behavior."

2. Preuss 1921-23, 2:692 (my English trans.).

3. For a detailed discussion of Uitoto kinship see: Jürg Gasché 1977, and Eugene and Dorothy Minor 1980.

4. Thomas Whiffen, at the beginning of the century, similarly observed: "No Indian ever uses his name, nor is he called by it when spoken to by his companions. One will speak to another as . . *Moɨma,* that is 'father' [or] in the case of a woman . . *Rinyo,* which is 'mother' . . . They will never address each other in more direct fashion, and if one of

the speakers is not a member of the household, and therefore no relationship exists between them, they will make use of some expression equivalent to our 'comrade,' 'man,' 'girl,' or other generality." (Whiffen 1915,-153-154) (*rinyo [riño]* means "woman"; *eiño* means "mother.")

5. Gerardo Reichel-Dolmatoff, in his work on Desana basketry, alleges that all aspects of Desana weaving—from raw materials to technology and actual patterns—are embedded in a symbolism of sex, food, marriage, and exogamy: "The weaving of basketry is a Desana metaphor for the life process, for sex, kinship, and food." (Reichel 1985, 25) "The common term for "to weave" [in Desana] is *suári,* but the alternative meanings for this verb are 'to interweave, to interpenetrate, to copulate, to intermarry.' *In other words, the entire weaving process symbolizes exogamous marriage patterns."* (Ibid., 27, emphasis added)

6. I use Reichel-Dolmatoff's terms to describe the basic techniques of basketry: "A first distinction must be made between a *passive* element which forms the more or less rigid foundation and a *moving* element which intertwines the first. I refer to the first element as *standard,* and to the second as *thread,* in the sense of warp and weft, respectively" (1985, 7-8).

7. For the groups of the Caquetá river basin, Maria C. van der Hammen (1992, 173) notes that: "In the same way that a predefined place of origin corresponded to each ethnic group, cultivated plants were given to them in such a way that a determinate set was assigned to each. Not all groups grow the same plants." So, according to her, *yagé* belongs to the Tukano-speaking groups (except those of the Mirití river), sugarcane to some of the Makuna, pineapple and peach palm to the Yukuna, yellow *umari* to the Uitoto. "Pursuing this direction further," she goes on, "a very clear relation between cultivated crop diversity and ethnic groups could be defined in the whole shamanistic macrospace." (My English trans.)

Text 3B

1. Fire, that is, rage.

2. The giant anteater's tail is almost as large as its body and has a thick coat of fur.

3. The Bora Indians live mainly in the lower Igaraparaná river and are neighbors of the Okaina and Uitoto.

4. *Yaripa:* one of several palm species employed in the construction of houses; see appendix 3.

5. *Compadre* (Spanish): godfather or father (in relation to one another). Abbreviated as *"compa."*

6. Mánaɨdɨkɨ: famous shaman from the upper Igaraparaná river.

Commentary on Text 3B

1. *Maloca:* large communal house of circular shape where the dance rituals are performed.

2. *Buinaima* is a title given to a person of honor or wisdom. The masters of dance rituals usually add the title Buinaima to their ritual names. The term *buinaima* is associated with water, and so it is said that the *buinaima*'s heart is as cool as water. The

fresh-water dolphin is also called *buinaima.*

Preuss notes the following in relation to this term: "An aquatic serpent; one of the mythical primates that lived in the water; persons who possess specific magical powers; beings that pierce holes; surname of the ancestors and beings of the netherworld; . . . sage, knower of something" (1921-23, 2:687-688, my English trans.).

3. In the Word of dancing rituals, the master refers to the people as *kue uruki,* which can be translated as "my children."

4. See commentary on text 3 where the topic of the "proper woman" is discussed in more detail.

Text 4

1. Cassava bread is made out of cassava meal and baked on the griddle. Cassava cakes are also made with cassava meal plus water and baked on the griddle; they are softer and fluffier. Cassava tamales are manioc dough wrapped in leaves and cooked in water.

Commentary on Text 4

1. The stem *zuui-* plus the affix *-ta-* ("to cause to") produces the verb *zuitade* which has three related meanings: (1) in a material sense it means "to unfasten (a knot), to untangle"; (2) in a physiological sense, it means that an illness has reached a critical point and is "released" in fever and sweat (a spell to treat high fever, for instance, is called *zuitárako jɨɨra); and* (3) in a psychic sense, it means "to relieve, to open up," as when it is said that a good coca *"komekɨ zuitade,"* "relieves the heart, opens up the mind."

By adding the affix *-ri-* ("duration, repetition") to *zuitade* we obtain the verb *zuirítate,* "to soften"—for instance, when a dry and stiff vine is put in water in order to make it soft and flexible.

2. In the Word on Discipline the relations of alliance are established by the man, who weaves the baskets for his wife; and here it seems that it is the father-in-law—the husband's father—who weaves the baskets. However, this contradiction is only apparent because alliance is here referred to in metaphorical terms. As the man and his father belong to the same filiation group (tribe or clan) the metaphorical sense of the basket offered to the woman does not change.

3. This expression is a remnant of older times when young men and women who were captured at war were allowed to live with the captor group, not as prisoners but as orphans. They could even get married within the group but they did not acquire full rights as the "proper" people. Nowadays, many elders use to say, "We are all orphans," because after the period of rubber exploitation many clans lost their shamans and chiefs and went to live with other groups, or next to the white people, as orphans.

4. The "proper" clan is the clan of the Miriti Palm Grove, or *Kɨnéreni,* to which Kɨneraɨ and his family belong.

Text 5

1. Fiber of *Ischnosiphon aruma* employed for weaving basketry, mainly strainers.

2. Fiber of the palm *Oenocarpus bacaba* (= *Jessenia bacaba)* employed to weave basketry, usually in conjunction with guarumo.

COMMENTARY ON TEXT 5

1. In this respect, the anthropologist Maria Cecilia López writes: "There are many prescriptions and recommendations about bathing. Children are taught not to be lazy; the mother submerges herself in the water with the small child while whispering advice into his ear, telling him that the Indian's life is not easy, that it requires a lot of strength and courage. The early-morning bath prevents one from aging and becoming gray-haired and "arthritic"; for this reason they must submerge themselves in the water before the yellow butterfly does and partake of the water's energy to keep healthy." (López 1993, 27)

2. Oscar Román, Uitoto from the Caquetá river (Colombian Amazon), told anthropologist Maria Cecilia López (1993, 43-44, emphasis added): "Evil, the negative, pain, illness—this feeling is transformed by Him, the Creator, into what is good and positive in nature, like the plants, the animals, the minerals and mankind. The latter is the purest form, the most 'crystalline'—prefigured as starch, *what is strained*—which appears in the form of various tribes."

3. Cf. the use of the verb "to be seated" *(ráitde)* in the commentary on text 3B.

4. In the myth "Story of the Creation" by the Uitoto Indian Octavio García (recorded by Fernando Urbina 1982), Buinaima, who is trying to free the people who are under the earth, tells his wife: "When people come yelling, *don't say a word,* because if you scream they will get scared and will return" (p. 10, emphasis added). Urbina, in a note, adds: "It is a custom among the Murui-Muinane [Uitoto] that when a person is seriously ill one should not raise one's voice in his presence because the person's spirit is travelling far away and can get scared and never return" (ibid.).

TEXT 6

1. *Biko,* literally "this shell"; it means "this body," "this *maloca* (communal house)," or "the firmament."

2. "House": *biko* (see note 1). It refers to the woman's body, and simultaneously refers to the community and the world.

TEXT 6A

1. Indians prepare the *yera* tobacco paste in this way: (1) they harvest mature tobacco leaves; (2) after rinsing the leaves, they boil them in water for several hours; (3) once the leaves are well cooked, they strain the whole mixture to obtain pure tobacco juice; (4) they cook this juice again, and when it is getting thick they add a plant to make it thicker and smoother (see "Source of tobacco mixture" in appendix 2); (5) they keep cooking it, stirring it constantly, until it obtains the right thickness of texture.

2. Indians prepare vegetable salt in the following way: (1) they collect the bark, flowers, buds, and other plant material from the various species from which salt is obtained (see "Source of vegetable salt" in appendix 2); (2) they burn this material until it is reduced to ashes; (3) they put the ashes in a piece of bark or heliconia leaf, with fern

273

leaves or moss at the bottom; (4) slowly, they filter water through the ashes, to precipitate the salts it contains; (5) they boil down the resulting water in order to dry the salts.

3. Indians prepare the coca powder or *mambe* in this way: (1) they harvest mature leaves of coca and put them to toast in a big clay pot or griddle; (2) they pound the toasted leaves in a wooden mortar so as to reduce them to powder; (3) they burn dry cecropia leaves to obtain ash; (4) they blend the pounded coca powder with the cecropia ashes and strain the blend using a fine piece of bark or cloth. They repeat the procedures of pounding, blending, and straining until only the veins and husk remain in the strainer.

4. The tobacco paste is stored in vessels called *yerafo*. Nevertheless, a good amount of tobacco remains stuck in the pot where it is prepared; this is called *iko ero* ("stuck to the bottom"). They add vegetable salt to this *iko ero,* and in this way they taste the new tobacco.

5. *Dirimao:* a spreading plant of the Compositae family. It is cultivated near the houses and has medicinal uses. See also commentary on texts 6, 6A and 6B.

Text 6B

1. Medicinal plant (see note 5 to text 6A).

2. *Jaibiki:* basil *(Ocimum* sp.)

3. Herbaceous medicinal plant (indet.). See also note 4 to Commentary on texts 6, 6A and 6B.

Commentary on Texts 6, 6A and 6B

1. "To discipline oneself" is the translation of the Uitoto verb *fimaide.* This verb is applied to the fasting and restrictions a person must follow when undertaking certain activities (e.g. ingesting power substances, performing rituals) or undergoing special circumstances (e.g. being pregnant, having a child, and so forth). This "disciplining" includes restriction from certain foods, from anger, from sexual intercourse, from sleeping, from doing certain activities.

2. *Dirimao* is a plant of the Compositae family (Henao 1990). *Jaibiki:*, basil, is the Labiatae *Ocimum* sp.

References to the other four plants are found in Preuss and other authors. For instance: "*naimere,* also *naime,* a sweet herb, used as a magical remedy" (Preuss 1921-1923, 2:734); Cristina Garzón also mentions a "sweet herb" with the name *naimekia,* but does not provide the botanical identification (Garzón and Makuritofe 1992, 260).

On *nozekue,* Preuss writes: "plant to scare away illnesses, also used for sorcery" (1921-1923, 2:738), and "plant to invoke health, supposedly identical to the *hanako* tree" (1:357); "*nozeko*" also appears in the myth of the Sun and Moon; with this plant, Kaniyuyu cured Manaidejitoma's eyes (1:311). In a story entitled "The origin of plants," the Indian elder Rafael Enokayi relates: "Then, in a while, you go to your father, and I am going to give you some things of your father [Mongobuinaima's mother told her son] . . [Mongobuinaima] went and his father gave him that *notekue [nozekue],* a little herb to take illnesses out with your hands" (Garzón and Makuritofe 1992, 70). Henao (1990) writes: "*Nozekue,* cultivated around the dwelling places to give health to people. The leaves are cooked in the juice of sweet manioc and then this liquid is drunk." Henao, however, does not report its botanical identification.

On *yinakai* Preuss writes: "a cultivated plant from whose leaves an extract that serves as a remedy is prepared to keep people healthy" (1921-1923, 2:666); *yinakai* also appears in the first song of the *maguaré* (drums) ritual—the song of the axe (ibid.). Rafael Enokayɨ, in the same story cited above, mentions "Father Yinakɨkaiño" as "one of the four pillars of our descent" (Garzón and Makuritofe 1992, 80).

On *katubai,* I have not found references in the literature. Of this plant Kɨneraɨ says: "a little plant that smells nice," and his son Blas, "a plant with round leaves."

3. Usually, the healer does not sing the words of the spell but only whistles the melody. At the end, he always blows.

4. In Preuss, we find *"Hirue Buineisai [Jírue Buinaizaɨ],* people of *Hirue,* a kind of fish" (1921-1923, 2:711). In the translation of Preuss' book into Spanish by Eudocio Becerra (Bigɨdɨma) and Gabriele Petersen de Piñeros, "Jirue Buineima" is glossed as "male mythical character, the 'Alga-*buineima'*" (Preuss 1994: 2:844).

The ending *-rue* in *jírue* is an archaic suffix that means "living being"; the nominal radical *ji-* is associated with liquids: it is the same root that, apparently, is found in the verb *jirode* "to drink."

5. Also, the verb *riéronaite* means "to be covered by dew."

Text 7

1. *jɨdokuiñoirɨ,* "bat plant"; this means "sweet potato," according to Kɨneraɨ. The common name for sweet potato is *refɨo.*

2. *uajɨ,* "the true tuber," a way of calling the bitter manioc *jujɨ.*

Commentary on Text 7

1. Appendix 1 lists the Uitoto names of cultivated species with their different suffixes for "plant," "stem," "leaf," "seed," "fruit," and so forth.

Text 8

1. The three activities of splitting, straining, and broadcasting refer to the preparation and sowing of the tobacco seeds. See commentary on texts 8 and 8A.

2. He refers here to the plant *jifíkona,* the leaves of which are used to prepare an extract to conjure the eyes with magic powers in order to see what is hidden. See text 8A and commentary on texts 8 and 8A.

Text 8A

1. *Jifíkona* is a small cultivated tree, about one and a half meters high. A sample, collected by biologist Olga L. Montenegro, was classified as the Apocynaceae *Bonafousia tetrastachya.* Its name is almost identical to that of the sapote tree:*jɨfikona* (only the accent changes). To conjure the eyes, fresh leaves of *jifíkona* are wrapped in a leaf of heliconia with some water, put next to the fire to cook for awhile, and then two drops of the liquid are sprinkled over each eye. That is why Kɨneraɨ uses the verb *daite,* which I translate as "to conjure," which literally means "to sprinkle, to spray."

Constanza La Rotta, in her study of Miraña ethnobotany, writes about this species: "The sap is applied to the eyes to clear the sight and to succeed in hunting." (La Rotta n.d.: 84) It is significant that in the Miraña language—as in Uitoto—the name of this plant, *mudsese,* is very similar to the name of the sapote tree.

2. Kɨnerai says that when the drops are applied, the affected person feels a strong pain in the eyes. If he does not discipline himself he will have suffered the pain in vain because the drug will have no effect or can seriously damage the eyes—as is the case in this story.

3. *Enókaizaɨ* is a Uitoto clan—of yellow soil *enoka*—from the Putumayo river.

4. The Putumayo river.

5. That is, he withdrew the *jifíkona* power by means of a spell.

COMMENTARY ON TEXTS 8 AND 8A

1. The procedure to extract vegetable salt can be found in note 2 to text 6A.

2. See note 1 to text 8A.

3. Or also "Heart That Tells the Things of the Ancients." Preuss (1921-1923: 2:694-695) interprets *yonera* as "narration, name of the ancients," and *yoneri* as "narrator, guardian spirit."

4. *Jafíraikɨ,* literally "Heart of Tranquility." I translate it as "of the Beginning of the World" because it refers to the tranquillity of the world when it was still covered by water.

TEXT 9

1. *Buinaima:* sage. See commentary on text 9, and note 2 to commentary on text 3B.

2. With tobacco and coca.

3. By saying that the "genuine" plants of tobacco, sweet manioc, and peanut are born, he is saying that children are born, both male (coca) and female (sweet manioc and peanut).

4. That is, the one who *mambes* but does not grow and prepare coca.

BIBLIOGRAPHY

Cardenal, Ernesto. 1979. *Antología de poesía primitiva.* Madrid: Alianza Editorial.

Casement, Sir Roger. 1911. "The Casement Report." In Hardenburg 1912, 264-338.

Domínguez, Camilo, and Augusto Gómez. 1994. *Nación y etnias: Conflictos territoriales en la Amazonia colombiana, 1750-1933.* Santafé de Bogotá: Coama and Disloque Editores.

Garzón, Cristina, and Vicente Makuritofe. 1992. *La noche, las plantas y sus dueños: Aproximación al conocimiento botánico en una cultura amazónica.* Bogotá: Corporación Colombiana para la Amazonia—Araracuara.

Gasché, Jürg. 1975. "Le système cultural Witoto." In *Amazonie Nord-Ouest,* ed. by J. Gabus, 111-128. Neuchâtel: Musée d'Ethnographie de Neuchâtel.

————. 1977. "Les fondements de l'organization sociale des indiens witoto et l'illusion exogamique." In *Actes du XLIIe Congrés International des Américanistes,* 2:141-161.

Hardenburg, W.E. 1912. *The Putumayo the Devil's Paradise: Travels in the Peruvian Amazon Region and an Account of the Atrocities Committed upon the Indians Therein,* edited and with an introduction by C.R. Enock. London: T. Fisher Unwin.

Henao, Clara Inés. 1990. "Interpretación etnobotánica del mito del 'árbol de las frutas' en la tradición oral huitoto como modelo de domesticación de las plantas en La Chorrera (Amazonas)." Thesis in Biology, Universidad Javeriana, Bogotá.

Hugh-Jones, Christine. 1979. *From the Milk River: Spatial and Temporal Processes in Northwest Amazonia.* Cambridge: Cambridge University Press.

Hymes, Dell. 1981. *"In Vain I Tried to Tell You": Essays in Native American Ethnopoetics.* Philadelphia: University of Pennsylvania Press.

Koch-Grünberg, Theodor. 1906. "Les indiens ouitoto: étude linguistique." *Journal de la Societé des Americanistes* Nouvelle Serie 3: 157-189.

Konɨraga, Toɨrabuinaima ie Juzigɨtofe. 1988. *Daɨ uzuma yote == Así contó el viejito,* compiled by P. Daniel Restrepo, trans. by Coowaho Dujdulli. La Chorrera (Amazonas, Colombia): Internado Sta. Teresita del Niño Jesús (mimeo).

Kricher, John C. 1989. *A Neotropical Companion: An Introduction to the Animals, Plants, and Ecosystems of the New World Tropics*. Princeton, NJ: Princeton University Press.

La Rotta, Constanza. n.d. *Especies utilizadas por la comunidad miraña: Estudio etnobotánico*. Bogotá: World Wildlife Fund and Fen-Colombia.

López, Maria Cecilia. 1993. *La maloca y el territorio*, módulo de Ciencias Sociales, Programa de Profesionalización de Maestros Indígenas, La Chorrera, Amazonas. Santafé de Bogotá: Fundación Etnollano.

Minor, Eugene A., and Dorothy Minor. 1980. "Sistema huitoto de parentesco." *Artículos en Lingüística y Campos Afines*, no. 8 (June): 67-91.

————. 1982. *Gramática pedagógica huitoto* Bogotá: Ministerio de Gobierno e Instituto Lingüístico de Verano.

————, comps. 1987. *Vocabulario bilingüe huitoto-español, español-huitoto (dialecto minica)*. Lomalinda, Meta: Ed. Townsend.

Pineda Camacho, Roberto. 1987. "Witoto." In *Introducción a la Colombia Amerindia*, 151-164. Bogotá: Instituto Colombiano de Antropología.

Preuss, Konrad Theodor. 1921-1923. *Religion und Mythologie der Uitoto: Textaufnahmen und Beobachtungen bei einem Indianerstamm in Kolumbien, Südamerika*, 2 vols. Göttingen and Leipzig: Vandenhoeck & Ruprecht and J.C. Hinrichs'sche.

————. 1994. *Religión y mitología de los Uitoto: Recopilación de textos y observaciones efectuadas en una tribu indígena de Colombia, Suramérica*, 2 vols, trans. by Ricardo Castañeda Nieto, Gabriele Petersen de Piñeros, and Eudocio Becerra. Santafé de Bogotá: Ed. Universidad Nacional, Instituto Colombiano de Antropología, Corporación Colombiana para la Amazonia Araracuara.

Reichel-Dolmatoff, Gerardo. 1985. *Basketry as Metaphor: Arts and Crafts of the Desana Indians of the Northwest Amazon*. Occasional Papers of the Museum of Cultural History, University of California, Los Angeles, no. 5.

Roldán Ortega, Roque. 1993. "Reconocimiento legal de tierras indígenas en Colombia." In *Reconocimiento y demarcación de territorios indígenas en la Amazonia: La experiencia de los países de la región*, 56-83. Bogotá: Cerec and Gaia Foundation.

Salick, Joe. 1989. "Ecological Basis of Amuesha Agriculture, Peruvian Upper Amazon." In *Resource Management in Amazonia: Indigenous and Folk Strategies*, edited by D.A. Posey and W. Balley, 189-212. New York: The New York Botanical Garden.

Sherzer, Joel. 1990. *Verbal Art in San Blas: Kuna Culture Through Its Discourse*. Cambridge: Cambridge University Press.

Steward, Julian H. 1948. "The Witotoan Tribes." In *Handbook of South American Indians,* ed. by J.H. Steward, 3: 749-762. New York: Cooper Square Publishers (1963) (Smithsonian Institution, Bureau of American Ethnology, bulletin 143).

Swann, Brian, ed. 1992. *On the Translation of Native American Literatures.* Washington and London: Smithsonian.

Taussig, Michael. 1987. *Shamanism, Colonialism, and the Wild Man: A Study in Healing and Terror.* Chicago: The University of Chicago Press.

Tedlock, Dennis. 1983. *The Spoken Word and the Work of Interpretation.* Philadelphia: University of Pennsylvania Press.

Urbina, Fernando. 1982. *Mitología amazónica: Cuatro mitos de los Murui-Muinanes.* Bogotá: Universidad Nacional.

van der Hammen, Maria Clara. 1992. *El manejo del mundo: Naturaleza y sociedad entre los Yukuna de la Amazonia colombiana.* Estudios en la Amazonia Colombiana, IV. Santafé de Bogotá: Tropenbos Colombia.

Whiffen, Thomas. 1915. *The North-West Amazon: Notes of Some Months Spent Among Cannibal Tribes.* London: Constable and Co. Ltd.

INDEX

283

Related title from Themis Books:

THE FOREST WITHIN
The World-View of the Tukano Amazonian Indians

Gerardo Reichel-Dolmatoff

"THIS BEAUTIFUL BOOK teaches us how to see trees as we have never seen them before. In a remote corner of the Amazonian forest, trees are a cosmic prism through which everything known to the Tukano Indians is brilliantly refracted... It is a rare privilege to be invited to contemplate forest ecology through the eyes of forest dwellers." - *Professor Mary Douglas*

"A SUPERBLY DOCUMENTED yet highly readable little masterpiece... We can only hope that it will serve to stimulate greater interest in the rest of his remarkable writings and also to make many people question the current dogma that if tribal people, leading their normal way of life, do not destroy the environment they have inhabited for hundreds if not thousands of years, it is merely because they do not have access to the requisite technology." - *Edward Goldsmith*

The Forest Within gives a detailed portrait of how an aboriginal tribe of the remote Amazonian region understands the cosmic dimensions of its partnership with the rainforest. The author explores the world-view of the Tukano Indians: their view of the forest as part of the cosmos; the Master (Spirit Guardian) of the Animals; their complex and multi-dimensional bond with their environment; and their social and sexual restrictions in order to achieve ecological sustainability.

GERARDO REICHEL-DOLMATOFF, the world-renowned Colombian anthropologist, devoted the last years of his life to studying the Indian tribes of the North-West Amazon. One of his particular interests was the ethno-ecology of the Tukano Indians and especially the extraordinary manner in which they have adapted to living in their forest environments. Author of twenty books and numerous articles, *The Forest Within* was the last book he wrote before his death in 1994.

Published in association with the COAMA Programme, Colombia
and The Gaia Foundation, London

ISBN 0 9527302 0 0   £12.95 / US $19.95

Related title from Themis Books:

THE WAY
An Ecological World-View

Edward Goldsmith

'A unique, extraordinary and profoundly challenging book... Goldsmith's urgent and prophetic book is destined to disturb the dogmatic slumbers of all the conventional philosophies."
John Gray, Times Literary Supplement

"Goldsmith has written a masterpiece... Every writer of environmental philosophy from now on will have to take Goldsmith's work into account."
J. Donald Hughes, author of 'Ecology in Ancient Civilizations'

FIRST PUBLISHED IN 1992, *The Way* is the *magnum opus* of one of the most influential figures of the international Green movement. This new edition has been fully revised and incorporates a glossary, bibliography and index.

The Way first provides a radical critique of the 'world-view' of Modernism with which we have all been imbued, and whose role the author sees as being primarily to rationalize and legitimize economic development or 'progress'. This world-view is faithfully reflected in modern science, including theoretical biology (Darwin's natural selection being but the biological version of Adam Smith's 'invisible hand'), also in today's reductionist and mechanistic 'New Ecology', and—possibly even more so—in the social sciences, particularly modern economics.

The Way then presents the underlying principles of an ecological world-view which, for the author, must reflect the original 'chthonic' or earth-oriented religion of traditional societies. In terms of the latter, human welfare can only be assured by following the Way (the R'ta of Vedic India and the Tao of ancient China). It is by following the Way that the critical order of the 'Cosmos', of the natural world and of the human societies that it encompasses (all of which are organized on the same plan and governed by the same laws) can be maintained.

Discontinuities such as epidemics, droughts and floods are correctly seen as evidence that the society affected has diverted from the Way and that the critical order of the 'Cosmos' has been disrupted. The answer is to return to the Way, rather than divert still further from it by applying mega-technological expedients that can only further disrupt the order of the natural world.

The Ecological World-View based on this principle and proposed in *The Way*, is all-embracing and totally coherent. It is also consistent with a sustainable social behaviour pattern that satisfies real (biological, social, ecological and spiritual) needs.

ISBN 0 9527302 3 5 £14.95 pb
ISBN 0 9527302 2 7 £25.00 hb